Access to Information, Technology, and Justice

BETA PHI MU SCHOLARS SERIES

Founded in 1948, Beta Phi Mu is the international library and information studies honor society. Its mission is to recognize and encourage scholastic achievement among library and information studies students.

The Beta Phi Mu Scholars series publishes significant contributions and substantive advances in the field of library and information science. Series editor Andrea Falcone is committed to presenting work which reflects Beta Phi Mu's commitments to scholarship, leadership, and service. The series fosters creative, innovative, and well-articulated works that members of the field will find influential.

Recently published titles in the series are:

Book Banning in 21st-Century America by Emily J. M. Knox
Young Adult Literature, Libraries, and Conservative Activism by Loretta M. Gaffney
School Librarianship: Past, Present, and Future Edited by Susan W. Alman
Six Issues Facing Libraries Today: Critical Perspectives by John Budd
Access to Information, Technology, and Justice: A Critical Intersection by Ursula Gorham

Access to Information, Technology, and Justice

A Critical Intersection

Ursula Gorham

ROWMAN & LITTLEFIELD
Lanham • Boulder • New York • London

Published by Rowman & Littlefield
A wholly owned subsidiary of The Rowman & Littlefield Publishing Group, Inc.
4501 Forbes Boulevard, Suite 200, Lanham, Maryland 20706
www.rowman.com

Unit A, Whitacre Mews, 26-34 Stannary Street, London SE11 4AB

British Library Cataloguing in Publication Information Available

Library of Congress Cataloging-in-Publication Data

Names: Gorham, Ursula, 1975- author.
Title: Access to information, technology, and justice : a critical intersection / Ursula Gorham.
Description: Lanham : Rowman & littlefield, [2017] | Series: Beta phi mu scholars series | Includes bibliographical references and index.
Identifiers: LCCN 2017007665 (print) | LCCN 2017007805 (ebook) | ISBN 9781442270299 (cloth : alk. paper) | ISBN 9781442270312 (electronic)
Subjects: LCSH: Technology and law. | Justice, Administration of—Automation. | Legal services—Automation. | Internet in legal services.
Classification: LCC K487.T4 G67 2017 (print) | LCC K487.T4 (ebook) | DDC 347.73/17—dc23
LC record available at https://lccn.loc.gov/2017007665

∞™ The paper used in this publication meets the minimum requirements of American National Standard for Information Sciences—Permanence of Paper for Printed Library Materials, ANSI/NISO Z39.48-1992.

Printed in the United States of America

To the Honorable Paul Mannes (1933–2016),
whose unwavering commitment to access to justice inspired me every day that I had the privilege to work alongside him

Contents

List of Figures and Tables

Acknowledgments

In late August 2015, Andrea Falcone, editor of the Beta Phi Mu Scholars Series, contacted me to inquire as to whether I would be interested in submitting a book proposal. This was barely four months after I had graduated with my Ph.D. from the University of Maryland College of Information Studies and, to be perfectly honest, I was enjoying my new focus on teaching and had doubts about whether it was the right time to commit to such a significant undertaking. A few conversations with Andrea were all it took to for me to realize that, even after four years of research and writing, I had more to say. And so I am deeply indebted to Andrea for this opportunity to expand my dissertation into a book and hopefully make a meaningful contribution to access to justice dialogues that are now more important than ever. I would also like to thank Charles Harmon at Rowman & Littlefield for walking me through the writing and editing process—his advice and recommendations undoubtedly improved the finished product. I feel incredibly fortunate to have worked with both Andrea and Charles—their guidance, enthusiasm, and encouragement over the past eighteen months have been invaluable.

I am also incredibly grateful for the support of my colleagues at the University of Maryland. Paul Jaeger, in particular, has been there every step of the way—his willingness to read the entire draft manuscript (after having read every word of my dissertation) is simply one of the many reasons why I consider myself fortunate to have him as a mentor and a friend.

My research on statewide legal information websites became a reality because of the support of Steve Anderson, Michael Craven, and Dave Pantzer of the Maryland State Law Library, Liz Keith of Pro Bono Net, and their wonderful colleagues. This study also would not have been possible without the willingness of the legal services providers and librarians to participate in surveys and interviews, patiently answering the many, many questions I had about their work. They continually inspired me with their passion for and commitment to their work—it has been a privilege to tell their stories.

On a personal note, I would like to thank my husband, Tony Oscilowski, and my parents, Peter and Ursula Gorham, for their unwavering love, support, advice, and encouragement as I have found my way in this world. Finally, I owe a tremendous debt of gratitude to my sons, Joseph and Dillon—each and every day, they make me laugh out loud, which is no easy feat when I've been writing and editing for hours on end. And, each and every day, their questions about the world around them inspire me to do what I can to advance the cause of social justice.

Introduction

In the fall of 2009, I found myself once again working at the United States Bankruptcy Court for the District of Maryland. As a law clerk, I was often the gatekeeper between individuals who had filed for bankruptcy and my judge. And, in this role as gatekeeper, I regularly found myself on the phone with individuals who were struggling to understand a court order, a motion filed by the bankruptcy trustee, or some other court document. As I was getting accustomed to this new role, I heard increased rumblings about how the recession was leading to unprecedented numbers of petitioners filing for bankruptcy without the benefit of legal counsel, or in legalese, pro se ("for oneself"). It then dawned on me that we were receiving these phone calls because people did not know where else to turn. During one of the most difficult times in their lives, they found themselves in the midst of a legal system that was complex and overwhelming.

I was sympathetic—and incredibly privileged to work alongside judges who were just as sympathetic and committed to ensuring that everyone who appeared before them had the opportunity to be heard. I wanted to be more than a sympathetic ear, though, and began thinking more and more about what needed to change. This led to the realization that what I was witnessing was part of a much larger phenomenon that was impacting our entire legal system. What I was witnessing was an overburdened system that was not designed to assist those without legal counsel and was thus unable to guarantee equal access to justice for an increasing number of people in this country.

Creating a system that offers equal access to justice to all who find themselves in it—not just those who are fortunate enough to have legal counsel—is not a matter of concern to the legal profession alone. Underlying our damaged legal system are inequities in income, education, literacy, and opportunity; fixing this system thus requires the attention and commitment of those working in a range of fields and institutions who understand the various ways in which these inequities intersect. And it requires the commitment of such individuals to build upon this understanding in pursuit of solutions to tackle this pressing societal problem.

This book is the culmination of the work I have undertaken over the past five and half years, since I left the bankruptcy court and began my doctoral studies at the University of Maryland College of Information Studies. I have been fortunate to study (and now work) in a program that embraces the view of access to information as a matter of social justice, and it is within this environment that I have been able to explore the intersection of access to justice, access to information, and technology.

ACCESS TO JUSTICE IN THE UNITED STATES

The United States Institute of Peace offers the following definition of access to justice:

> Access to justice is more than improving an individual's access to courts or guaranteeing legal representation. Access to justice is defined as the ability of people to seek and obtain a remedy through formal or informal institutions of justice for grievances in compliance with human rights standards. There is no access to justice where citizens (especially marginalized groups) fear the system, see it as alien, and do not access it; where the justice system is financially inaccessible; where individuals have no lawyers; where they do not have information or knowledge of rights; or where there is a weak justice system.

The concept of equal access to justice is generally touted as one of the foundations of the American legal system. As observed by Lewis Powell Jr., U.S. Supreme Court justice, during his tenure as president of the American Bar Association (ABA), "[e]qual justice under law is not merely a caption on the facade of the Supreme Court building, it is perhaps the most inspiring ideal of our society. It is one of the ends for which our entire legal system exists—it is fundamental that justice should be the same, in substance and availability, without regard to economic status." A significant gap, however, exists between our expressed commitment to this principle and the system in place now.

In 2017, far too many people living in the United States are denied access to justice. We are dealing with what is often considered to be a basic problem of supply and demand (Legal Services Corporation, 2012; Morris, 2013). The Legal Services Corporation (LSC), an independent non-profit corporation established by Congress in 1974, is the largest funder of civil legal services in America, distributing grants through a competitive process to various organizations that provide legal services to low-income populations and monitoring the organizations' use of those funds (Johnstone, 2011). Although Congress has appropriated $300–$400 million to LSC on an annual basis, LSC has never been fully able to achieve its goals due to inadequate resources. Nearly one in five Americans now qualifies for LSC-funded legal assistance (LSC, 2012). Moreover, a growing number of eligible individuals need legal assistance due to rising rates of foreclosures, bankruptcies, and unemployment in the wake of the recent global recession, as well as to regulatory changes in government benefit programs, such as Social Security, Medicaid, and public housing (Cohen, 2013; Jefferson, 2013; Staudt, 2013). The result is nothing short of alarming—at least 50 percent of eligible individuals who seek assistance from LSC-funded organizations are currently being turned away (LSC, 2012).

We are therefore left with a persistent "justice gap," defined by LSC as the "difference between the current level of legal assistance and the level which is necessary to meet the needs of low-income Americans" (LSC, 2007, p. 1). The justice gap is not, by any stretch of the imagination, a new problem, as there have always been individuals in this country who could not afford to obtain legal counsel. And there have never been enough state and federal government funds devoted to meeting this particular need. In recent years, however, the phenomenon of self-representation has taken on a life of its own, and the number of individuals representing themselves in certain types of cases—such as family law—is nothing less than staggering. One result has been the shining of a spotlight on the plight of those who are forced to navigate a complex legal system on their own. Examples of recent reports and studies investigating this issue include the following:

- Following a study of the self-represented litigants in family court in Oregon, Colorado, Tennessee, and Massachusetts, the Institute for the Advancement of the American Legal System developed a series of recommendations designed to help state courts better serve this population (2016)
- A study conducted on behalf of the New York City Bar Association's Pro Bono and Legal Services Committee found that the provision of free counsel to low-income tenants facing eviction would produce a net savings of $320 million for the city (Stout Risius Ross, 2016)

Moreover, in its 2017 budget request, the LSC provided statistics from judges' reports that highlighted the sheer volume of cases in which one or more parties were representing themselves. For example, in Arizona, 90 percent of litigants in domestic violence and probate cases are unrepresented, whereas in Hawaii, 96 percent of defendants in landlord-tenant cases and 80 percent of defendants in foreclosure actions are unrepresented (LSC, 2016a).

THE INTERSECTION OF ACCESS TO JUSTICE AND ACCESS TO INFORMATION

The ABA convened the Commission on the Future of Legal Services in 2014, tasking it with an investigation into "various reasons why meaningful access to legal services remains out of reach for too many Americans" (ABA, 2016, p. 1). The commission's final report, issued in August 2016, was dedicated to, among others, "the estimated 80 percent of the poor, and those of moderate means, without meaningful access to our justice system." Recognizing that "the goal of justice for all remains elusive," the commission urged the legal profession to support "the aspirational goal of 100 percent access to effective assistance for essential civil legal needs" (p. 37). The commission's development of financially viable models for delivering legal services involved an examination of the impact of technology, among other forces, currently transforming the society in which we live.

This examination was part of a larger movement in legal services to embrace self-help services as part of the solution to the justice gap. The concept of self-help in the legal arena also is not new—Nolo Press, for example, began publishing self-help legal books in the early 1970s with *How to Do Your Own Divorce in California*. The movement gained momentum when, at the turn of the twenty-first century, the Internet began paving the way for the rapid development and deployment of self-help applications through information and communication technologies (ICTs).

At around the same time as the ABA's initiative, LSC was convening the Summit on the Use of Technology to Expand Access to Justice. Through sessions held in June 2012 and January 2013, the summit brought together seventy-five leaders from various organizations involved in furthering access to justice (e.g., legal services, courts, libraries, and academia). Participants of the summit commenced work on a strategy for the creation of an integrated legal services delivery system,[1] a key component of which is a statewide access portal that will use an automated triage process to help those in need of legal assistance. In developing this strategy, the summit participants were guided by the following mission:

> To explore the potential of technology to move the United States toward providing some form of effective assistance to 100% of persons otherwise unable to afford an attorney for dealing with essential civil legal needs. (LSC, 2013, p. 1)

Already, the vision created by summit participants is being brought to life. In April 2016, the LSC, in partnership with Microsoft Corporation and Pro Bono Net, announced a new initiative to develop statewide legal portals. Through these portals, individuals with legal needs will be directed to the most appropriate form of assistance. The project will begin with the development of two portals, with the goal of replicating this approach throughout the country.

The envisioned portals represent an expansion of the statewide legal information websites that now exist throughout the United States. These websites have evolved from static collections of resources (often electronic versions of print materials) and basic links into dynamic websites that often incorporate multimedia content and interactive tools, such as automated legal form and document preparation systems. Situated at the intersection of access to justice and access to information, they are thus intended to serve as the proverbial giant upon whose shoulders a future legal services delivery system will be built.

This emerging understanding of the role that technology can play in expanding access to justice is an important step forward; however, more work needs to be done so that we can develop a clearer picture of whether these new initiatives are making a difference in the lives of individuals with unmet legal needs. The current lack of research in this area, however, is emblematic of a larger problem permeating the legal services community. As described by Rhode (2013):

> American legal aid lacks independent, well-developed research capacities. The Legal Services Corporation's Research Institute lost funding in the 1980s and has never been reestablished. Decision making often proceeds without reliable information about the amount, type, and funding of services provided, the dimensions and drivers of unmet needs and the relative effectiveness of different delivery models along multiple dimensions. Although we do not lack for studies on certain topics, much of the data we have is too limited in scope and methodology to supply a rational basis for policy making. And much of what we know is not presented or disseminated in ways that adequately inform delivery structures or political debates about subsidized legal services. (p. 533)

Charn and Selbin (2013) offer a similar assessment, noting that there has been insufficient empirical study of both demand-side issues (e.g., consumer needs, user preferences, and problem-solving behaviors) and supply-side issues (e.g., funding, services, quality, outcomes, accessibility, and cost effectiveness). In recent years, critics have increasingly focused on the lack of studies that examine the outcomes of access to justice initiatives (Birnbaum & Bala, 2012; Buhai, 2009; Rhode & Bam, 2012; Smith & Stratford, 2012; Steinberg, 2011). The lack of outcome data, it is argued, leads to an insufficient understanding of the efficacy of existing programs (Cantrell, 2002; Selbin, Charn, Alfieri, & Wizner, 2012; Smith, 2013). The absence of evaluative efforts has become increasingly problematic as, in the current policy environment, service providers are increasingly called upon to demonstrate the effectiveness of what they are doing to funding entities, decision makers, and the public (Aaron, 2012; Selbin et al., 2012). Rather than utilizing empirical methodologies typically employed in the social sciences for purposes of evaluation, however, policy decisions in the legal services realm typically rely heavily on anecdotal evidence focused on the success of individual programs (Cantrell, 2002; Engler, 2010). This approach does not necessarily lend itself to the creation of a body of knowledge that can inform the policy and practice of the access to the justice community as a whole (Abel, 2009; Blasi, 2004; Engler, 2010).

As might be expected, much of the legal services research that has been conducted has focused on the impact of practitioner representation, with comparatively less attention paid to legal self-help services (Rhode, 2013). The appeal of self-help services and other forms of limited assistance is clear—they allow more individuals to benefit from some level of legal assistance. But, as the initial focus has been largely on making these services available, the legal community has only recently begun to examine whether these services are meeting the needs of self-help users or are merely deemed acceptable due to the unavailability of representation to all who need it (Selbin et al., 2012). As articulated by Abel (2012),

> The spectrum of self-help services is a necessary innovation in light of the extreme shortage of counsel for low-income communities. At the same time, we lack an evidence base to determine the scope and efficacy of self-help services. Some worry that self-help services will provide the appearance of a solution to the *pro se* crisis when in fact *pro se* litigants still cannot effectively assert their claims. (p. 812)

With the notable exceptions of comprehensive overviews of self-represented litigant programs by Greacen (2011) and the Self-Represented Litigation Network (SRLN) (2008), as well as the SRLN's more recent study focused on the services that law libraries in the United States provide to self-represented litigants (2014), the emphasis on individual programs has contributed to the lack of cohesiveness that permeates this body of research in the United States (Greacen, 2002). As Richard Zorza, a prominent access to justice scholar, has noted, "the extensive innovation and experimentation that is going on in this field is largely uncoordinated and undirected. Innovators in one state often find it hard to discover what others have done, and what information that is available is usually focused on one program or innovation" (2007, p. 81). The result is that states are not taking full advantage of the opportunity to learn from one another through the sharing of best practices and lessons learned.

The network of statewide legal information websites now in existence throughout the United States is but one example of "the extensive innovation and experimentation" observed by Zorza. As noted above, they are the basis for the statewide portals envisioned in the LSC summit's final report. And, given the central role that they are likely to play in the delivery of legal services in the future, the time is undoubtedly ripe for a comprehensive assessment of these initiatives. In the past few years, significant progress has been made toward building a more holistic body of knowledge about statewide legal information websites. In addition to my dissertation research (which will be discussed throughout this book), Dyson and Schellenberg (2016) recently evaluated the readability of content available through the websites of legal aid organizations. Moreover, LSC, through a two-year grant from the Ford Foundation, has undertaken a project to assess the accessibility and usability of statewide legal information websites. As of the writing of this book, LSC had hired a consultant to assist with this evaluation study. The primary goal of this evaluation is to create

> a better understanding of the quality of resources available on the statewide website network, including what types of online resources and tools are available across the country and whether content is set up to meet the needs of low-income users. The planned evaluation will highlight both the strengths and weaknesses of the statewide website network. It will give all states a better understanding of how to improve their sites and replicate successful initiatives. (LSC, 2016b)

These two studies interject the notion of equitable access to information into access to justice dialogues. Both are grounded in the premise that it is not enough to use technology to disseminate information. The success—or lack thereof—of statewide legal information websites and related initiatives depends on the extent to which people can understand and use the information made available through these initiatives. As articulated by the Washington State Access to Justice Board in its "Access to Justice Technology Principles" (2004):

> Access to justice requires that the public have available understandable information about the justice system, its resources, and means of access. The justice system should promote ongoing public knowledge and understanding of the tools afforded by technology to access justice by developing and disseminating information and materials as broadly as possible in forms and by means that can reach the largest possible number and variety of people.

Unfortunately, however, opportunities arising from ICTs do not accrue to everyone equally, as physical, intellectual, and social barriers to information persist. Those who cannot read, those who do not speak the English language, those who are unfamiliar with the law, and those with limited digital literacy skills all find themselves at a fundamental disadvantage. For these individuals, access to ICTs alone provides neither equitable access to information nor equal access to justice. They require some sort of assistance to help them overcome what is often a series of interrelated barriers. And so the role of community-based organizations, such as non-profit organizations serving disadvantaged populations and public libraries, in helping those facing such barriers to information access remains as vital as ever.

By and large, legal professionals and information professionals have been separately examining access to justice and access to information, respectively. These two dialogues should not remain separate however, and the notion that equal access to justice requires equitable access to information deserves further exploration. This book thus seeks to add to the small but growing body of literature that focuses on the critical intersection of technology, access to justice, and access to information. It seeks to build upon existing work in this area by undertaking an in-depth exploration of how ICTs are changing—and failing to change—the legal information landscape for those who most need this information.

Using my dissertation research on statewide legal information websites as a case study, this book brings together the separate dialogues on legal self-help services in two principal ways:

- it suggests a new approach to examining online legal self-help services, using research from the fields of e-government and information studies to frame the information access issues raised by these services; and
- it encourages readers to think about the role that institutions outside of the legal system (e.g., public libraries) play in promoting access to justice and how this role can be expanded.

A NOTE ABOUT TERMINOLOGY

Before providing an overview of the book, a couple of observations about the terminology used throughout this book are in order. In the literature, as well as in practice, the users of self-help services and resources are often referred to as pro se or self-represented litigants. The State Justice Institute (SJI) defines a self-represented litigant as "[a] person (party) who advocates on his or her own behalf before a court, rather than being represented by an attorney" (2014). However, many individuals with legal needs never officially enter the legal system (Morris, 2013). This was demonstrated in a study by Sandefur of the civil justice experiences of the American public, in which she found that two-thirds of the sample experienced at least one civil justice situation (related to, for example, housing, employment, money, or insurance) in the preceding eighteen months (Sandefur, 2014). But, because these individuals rarely turn to lawyers or courts for help in handling these situations, they never become self-represented litigants. For that reason, this study generally adopts Morris's use of the term "self-help user" (p. 170). Many of the individuals who participated in the study detailed in chapters 4–7, however, use the term "self-represented litigant"; thus, that term appears throughout the book as well.

The concept of access to information requires an explanation for a different reason, namely, that it is more complex than may appear at first blush. This book discusses information access in terms of the tripartite model of access: physical, intellectual, and social (Burnett, Jaeger, & Thompson, 2008).

> *Physical access* is generally viewed as access to the document or other form embodying information, be it conveyed through print, electronic, verbal, or another means of communication—literally the process of getting to the information that is being sought (Svenonius, 2000). . . . *Intellectual access* can be understood as the accessing of the information itself after physical access has been obtained (Svenonius, 2000). It revolves around the ability to understand how to get to and, in particular, how to understand the information itself once it has been physically obtained. . . . [Social access] is the third and most abstract aspect of information access [that] captures the idea that, simply because one *can* physically and intellectually access needed information, it does not necessarily follow that they *do* access that information or that all users interpret the information in the same way. (Jaeger, Taylor, & Gorham, 2015)

It is of particular importance to keep this definition of information access in mind as we consider recent developments in the use of technology to address the persistent justice gap in this country.

STRUCTURE OF THE BOOK

Following this introductory chapter, the remainder of the book will address the issues discussed above in much greater detail, bringing together once separate dialogues on access to justice and access to information. The goal is to weave together research from the legal and information fields to offer a fresh perspective on how collaborative efforts among diverse community and government organizations can facilitate access to legal information by those who most need it.

Chapter 1 offers historical and current perspectives on the justice gap, setting the stage for this book's exploration of the intersection between access to justice and equitable access to information. This chapter will describe the growth of the access to justice community under the leadership of LSC, identifying key players in this community. Chapter 1 will close with a discussion of three strategies currently being pursued within the access to justice community to close the justice gap.

Chapter 2 sets up a key proposition of the book, namely, that access to information is an integral component of access to justice. For individuals navigating the legal system without the benefit of legal counsel, the ability to understand and use both substantive and procedural legal information is crucial. As explored in this chapter, however, many members of traditionally underserved populations are struggling to overcome a complex and interconnected set of barriers to information access in this environment. Chapter 2 concludes with a description of the efforts of courts, legal aid and other community organizations, and libraries to develop self-help resources and programs designed to dismantle these barriers to information access.

Chapter 3 focuses on technological advancements in the past twenty years that have created new avenues for closing the justice gap. Websites and online tools created by courts and legal organizations for self-help users are discussed in this chapter. This chapter also describes the difficulty that many self-help users face when attempting to use these websites and tools due to limited literacy skills, raising questions about the extent to which technological advancements have dismantled long-standing barriers to information faced by underserved populations.

Chapters 4 and 5 present a case study of statewide legal information websites. Chapter 4 describes the evolution of the existing network of statewide legal information websites over the past twenty years and reviews research and best practices in this area. Chapter 5, after providing an overview of my recent study of statewide legal information websites, presents key survey and interview findings that explore the intersection of access to justice and equitable access to information within this specific context.

Chapter 6 presents an in-depth exploration of one key finding from the case study presented in chapters 4 and 5: the role of collaboration in facilitating access to information via statewide legal information websites. This chapter will discuss the different forms that collaboration takes in this environment, highlighting how legal aid organizations, libraries, government agencies, and other community organizations each play an important role in leveling the information playing field for underserved populations. Detailed descriptions of a number of innovative collaborative efforts currently taking place across the United States (identified through the case study but not limited to statewide legal information websites) provide the framework for this discussion.

And, lastly, recommendations for policy and practice are set forth in chapter 7. Building upon findings from the case study, this chapter explores ways in which we can learn more about whether the existing programs and services discussed throughout this book do, in fact, advance access to justice. Toward that end, it provides a framework for user-centered evaluation. An important component of this framework is ongoing collaboration among the diverse groups that now make up the access to justice community. Accordingly, suggestions for fostering collaboration among these groups are included as well.

Given that this book covers much new ground in bringing together strands from several distinct bodies of literature and presenting research that sits squarely at the intersection of access to information and access to justice, it has been written to be widely accessible to both practitioners and scholars in the legal and information fields. It is intended to be a resource for individuals working in a diverse array of settings, including public libraries, law school clinics and libraries, courthouses, providers of legal services, and advocacy organizations. It is worth noting that legal problems, if left unaddressed, often have widespread repercussions. As described by Gershbain (2016), "[i]gnoring or abandoning a legal problem not only means someone's rights don't get vindicated: unresolved legal issues tend to spiral and create other social problems. Left untreated, legal problems can create mental illness, health issues, loss of employment, relationship breakdown, precarious housing, bankruptcy, violence, loss of custody, and homelessness." With this in mind, the book is also written to be a resource for providers of social services who, in many cases, are already collaborating with members of the access to justice community and libraries to better meet the varied needs of the populations they serve.

The ideas and suggestions in this book hopefully will help members of each of these communities to better understand how equitable access to information facilitates access to justice and the role of technology in fostering these developments. This enhanced understanding, in turn, will help professionals improve upon the services they provide as part of their ongoing efforts to assist individuals with unmet legal needs. As bringing together these dialogues is only the first step, the book also serves as an invitation for other researchers and scholars to explore the connections between equitable access to information and equal access to justice. The next chapter begins this exploration with an in-depth examination of the justice gap, the emergence of which created the need for the innovations discussed throughout this book.

NOTE

1. The other enumerated components of the strategy are document assembly, mobile technologies, business process analysis, and expert systems.

List of Abbreviations

Affordable Care Act	ACA
American Association of Law Libraries	AALL
American Bar Association	ABA
Community-based participatory research	CBPR
Federal Communications Commission	FCC
Information and communication technologies	ICTs
Interest on Lawyer Trust Accounts	IOLTA
LawHelp Interactive	LHI
Legal Services Corporation	LSC
Legal Services National Technology Assistance Project	LSNTAP
Limited English proficiency	LEP
National Center for State Courts	NCSC
National Telecommunications and Information Administration	NTIA
Open Source Template	OST
Participatory action research	PAR
People's Law Library	PLL
Self-Represented Litigation Network	SRLN
State Justice Institute	SJI
Technology Initiative Grants	TIG

1

The Emergence of a Justice Gap

In the United States, the intersection of information, technology, and the law can be traced to an overburdened legal system. The concept of equal access to justice reflects the ideal that the legal system leads to "results that are individually and socially just" (American Association of Law Libraries [AALL], 2014, p. 5 [quoting Cappelletti and Garth, 1978]). It is generally touted as one of the foundations of the American legal system and "can be found in the language of the U.S. constitution, the political philosophy underlying the U.S. constitution, and the common law legal tradition from which the U.S. legal system sprung" (Johnson, 2000). For the reasons explored in this chapter, however, the concept of equal access to justice has yet to be fully realized.

We know that the civil legal services delivery system in the United States is failing for many, as evidenced by reports that 80 percent of the civil legal needs of the poor go unmet (Engler, 2011; Houseman, 2001; Landsman, 2009; LSC, 2009; Spieler, 2013).[1] This figure is frequently uttered, and yet it stands in sharp contrast to prevailing perceptions about access to counsel in civil cases. Nearly four out of five Americans erroneously believe that a right to counsel exists in civil cases, and only one-third of Americans believe that low-income individuals would have difficulty obtaining legal assistance (Rhode, 2004). It is worth examining each of these perceptions in a little more depth.

THE EMERGENCE OF A JUSTICE GAP

At the core of the American legal system are lawyers, who are depended upon not only to provide a voice for their clients but also to use their legal knowledge and case management experience to keep the system running smoothly (Zimerman & Tyler,

2010). In reality, though, lawyers may not be at the center of every legal case. Self-representation—like equal access to justice—is a defining characteristic of the American legal system (Schwarz, 2004; Swank, 2004). The right to be heard, guaranteed by the Sixth Amendment, lays the foundation for the right of self-representation. It was initially codified by the Judiciary Act of 1789, and later in 28 U.S.C. § 1654 (1994). Underlying this right is the belief that "all individuals, no matter their status or wealth, are entitled to air grievances for which they may be entitled to relief. Access, then, must not be contingent upon retaining counsel, lest the entitlement become a mere privilege denied to certain segments of society" (Schneider, 2011, p. 586). In other words, the right to have one's day in court is not dependent upon one's ability to obtain legal counsel (Zimerman & Tyler, 2010).

Few believe, however, that access to the courts is synonymous with access to justice, as evidenced by the ongoing debate surrounding the right to counsel. In *Gideon v. Wainwright*, 372 U.S. 335 (1963), the U.S. Supreme Court ruled that, under the Fourteenth Amendment to the U.S. Constitution, state courts are required to provide defense attorneys to indigent criminal defendants. Under federal law, however, there is no equivalent right to counsel in civil cases. In *Lassiter v. Department of Social Services of Durham County, North Carolina* (1981), a divided Supreme Court held that there was a presumption against the right to counsel in civil cases unless the loss of physical liberty was at stake (Lidman, 2006). The right to counsel in civil cases is not guaranteed under state law either, with only a limited number of states recognizing it under narrowly defined circumstances, generally related to the protection of minors (Johnson, 2000).

The absence of a civil right to counsel enabled the emergence of the so-called justice gap, or the "difference between the current level of legal assistance and the level which is necessary to meet the needs of low-income Americans" (LSC, 2007, p. 1). Efforts to address this imbalance can be traced to the late nineteenth century, when the first civil legal assistance program opened its doors in New York City (Lang, 2011). Similar programs began appearing in major cities throughout the country, leading to a patchwork of programs wholly dependent on private charities. The federal government's first steps into the delivery of civil legal services occurred with an Office of Economic Opportunity program financed through War on Poverty legislation in the 1960s. The purpose of this program was "to have legal services lawyers for the poor do no less for their clients than does the corporation lawyer checking the Federal Trade Commission for sloppy rulemaking, the union lawyer asking Congress for repeal of 14(b), or the civil rights lawyer seeking an end to segregation in bus stations" (Rulli, 2011, p. 684).

Through the subsequent establishment of the LSC, Congress brought attention to "the need to provide equal access to the system of justice in our nation for those who would be otherwise unable to afford adequate legal counsel" (LSC, 2009). LSC grantees generally provide legal services in the areas of family law (e.g., divorce, custody, and domestic violence), housing, and consumer issues (Staudt, 2009). As the U.S. legal aid system under LSC began to take shape, it became defined by the presence of legal professionals (both attorneys and paralegals) committed to poverty law, as well as by grantees' growing role in law reform and other advocacy efforts (Menkel-Meadow, 1984).

LSC was initially the beneficiary of steady increases in federal funding, with its budget growing to $321 million within the first five years of its existence (Johnson, 2009). Since then, however, LSC has experienced repeated and significant budget cuts (Smith & Stratford, 2012), never returning to its earliest funding levels in real, inflation-adjusted dollars (Johnson, 2009). In fact, when inflation is taken into account, LSC funding has dropped by one-third over the past fifteen years (Rhode & Bam, 2012). Numbers reported by the LSC confirm the extent to which these cuts dramatically impact services: "In 2010, when LSC received its largest appropriation in absolute dollars, grantees provided services to 2.3 million people in all households served. Four years later, after LSC's appropriations fell, LSC grantees were able to help only 1.9 million people in all households served, a decline of 17 percent" (LSC, 2016a).

During the 1990s, these budgetary cuts were also coupled with reform efforts that led to restrictions in terms of the clients that LSC-funded organizations could serve and the types of cases they could take (Rhode, 2009). Notable restrictions imposed at that time include a ban on class action lawsuits and the litigation of cases involving abortion. In response to these restrictions, many legal aid providers opted to forego LSC funds and began to search for alternative sources of funding (Lang, 2011). Twenty years later, the budgetary situation for LSC-funded organizations remains bleak, further aggravated by the absence of political clout on the part of individuals with civil legal needs who cannot afford counsel. This lack of influence and voice is due to this population's inability to develop any cohesive group identity (Snukals & Sturtevant, 2007).

While LSC and its grantee organizations find themselves operating in an increasingly constrained resource environment, the demand for their services is as great as ever. As noted in the introduction, nearly one in five Americans now qualifies for LSC-funded legal assistance (LSC, 2012). In general, the maximum income level for legal aid eligibility is 125 percent of the Federal Poverty Guidelines promulgated by the Department of Health and Human Services (Legal Services Corporation 2015 Income Guidelines). As noted in LSC's 2017 budget request, a household with four members in the continental United States must have its total income below $30,375 in order to qualify for legal aid assistance. Recent U.S. Census Bureau figures reveal that, in 2014, sixty-three million people fell below this income threshold (LSC, 2016a). Of those who qualify for legal assistance, 6.5 million (10.3 percent) were seniors sixty-five years of age or older and 11.6 million (18.4 percent) were persons with disabilities (LSC, 2016a).

Moreover, as noted by Berenson (2001), the majority of Americans—those who fall between the poorest 20 percent of the population (who qualify for legal aid) and the richest 10 percent (who can afford to pay for legal representation)—have unmet legal needs. Thus, there is growing awareness that moderate-income individuals, as well as those who qualify for legal aid under the federal guidelines, all too often find themselves caught in the justice gap; recent statistics indicating that from 40 to 60 percent of the legal needs of middle-income individuals go unmet shed light on a rarely acknowledged facet of the justice gap (Landsman, 2009; National Center for State Courts [NCSC], 2006; Spieler, 2013; see also Rhode [2009] and Haddon [2014]).

This growth in demand for services—coupled with the pressure of diminishing resources—has placed the legal services community in an untenable position. "To borrow a health services analogy, the United States is in a 'triage' situation—indeed one of 'extreme triage'—trying to pick the relative few poor people to which its limited legal service resource will be able to offer a free lawyer" (Johnson, 2000). Both the percentage of attorneys providing civil legal services (less than 1 percent of U.S. attorneys) and the budgets for which these attorneys work (less than one-half of 1 percent of total expenditures on attorneys in the United States) are small fractions of what is required to meet current demand (Johnson, 2009; Rhode, 2004). Per LSC, there is one legal aid attorney available for every 6,415 individuals living in this country, and at least 50 percent of eligible individuals who seek assistance from LSC-funded organizations are currently being turned away (LSC, 2012). A recent report discussing the justice gap in Florida, for example, revealed that, among people facing a legal problem in the past year, only 16 percent of them had received legal assistance. Similarly, "[a] Washington State Supreme Court report released last year found that 70 percent of low-income households in Washington faced a significant civil legal issue in the past 12 months, but three-fourths did not seek or could not obtain legal assistance" (LSC, 2016a).

Studies from around the country document equally disheartening justice gaps (LSC, 2016a):

- In Massachusetts, as reported by the Boston Bar Association, the number of people being turned away from legal services providers has increased since 2006, from 50 percent to 64 percent.
- In Michigan, 19 percent fewer cases were handled between 2011 and 2013 after budget cuts led to the closure of two offices and the layoff of forty-nine staff members.

The harsh reality facing those individuals who qualify for legal assistance stands in sharp contrast to the situation in which individuals who can hire an attorney find themselves—there is one private attorney available for every 429 individuals who do not qualify for legal aid under the Federal Poverty Guidelines (LSC, 2009). A dichotomy in legal practice is now emerging wherein there is too little litigation by those with valid legal claims but without the financial means to obtain counsel and too much litigation by those with the financial means to pursue frivolous claims (Glater, 2006).

The Washington State Supreme Court report mentioned earlier highlights yet another underexplored facet of the justice gap: the fact that there are many people with legal needs who do not seek assistance from legal services providers. As Rhode (2013) suggests, the justice gap thus may be even greater than it appears at first blush: "Surveys documenting the numbers of eligible individuals turned away by legal aid offices give no indication of the much larger number with legal problems who fail to contact providers because of disability, language barriers, geographic isolation, insufficient information or lack of confidence in the value of seeking assistance" (p. 534). The fact that we do not have a clear and accurate picture of the full extent of the justice gap is perhaps even more troubling than the figures and statistics already recited.

OVERVIEW OF CIVIL LEGAL SERVICES IN THE UNITED STATES

Although we may lack a full understanding of the scope of the justice gap, we have a somewhat better understanding of the current system in place that is tirelessly working to close this gap. As of 2011, there were approximately five hundred independent providers of legal services. One hundred thirty-six of them are funded by LSC (Houseman, 2011). Many of these providers are small-scale public-private partnerships (Sandefur & Smyth, 2011). Some programs focus on specific populations (e.g., the elderly, veterans, individuals with HIV or AIDS), while others provide services to the general public. Among the services they provide are advice, community legal education, and policy advocacy. There are an additional nine hundred pro bono programs operating in this system, as well as two hundred law school clinical programs, several hundred self-help programs, and twenty state support organizations that provide training and technical support to local providers (Houseman, 2011). Looking across the vast network, "[w]hile funders do make some restrictions, the legal aid programs themselves generally make key decisions about the area and client base they will serve, the mix of staff they employ, and the scope and type of services they will provide" (Houseman, 2011). The existing infrastructure reflects "a fundamental absence of coordination in the system, fragmentation and inequality in who gets served and how, and arbitrariness in access to justice depending on where one lives" (Sandefur & Smyth, 2011).

The total amount of expenditures in this area is difficult to gauge precisely because of the fragmented nature of the system (Houseman, 2011). Per Sandefur and Smyth (2011), however, total public and private funding for legal aid in 2009 was approximately $1.3 billion. As they note, though, "[w]hile over a billion dollars is in some ways a substantial expenditure, the amount is small when compared to total public spending on justice-related activities. In 2007, federal, state, and local governments spent an estimated $228 billion for police protection, corrections, and judicial and legal services (Bureau of Justice Statistics 2011)" (p. 17). It is important to note that this figure also includes alternative sources of funding, including Interest on Lawyer Trust Accounts (IOLTA) programs[2] and private organizations (Johnson, 2009; Lang, 2011; Rhode, 2009). Recognizing IOLTA programs as an important source of funding for civil legal aid and other initiatives, states have made a concerted effort to bolster these programs. Forty-four states, for example, now prohibit lawyers from opting out of IOLTA programs. In addition, a number of states have adopted measures to limit the fees that can be charged on IOLTA accounts and/or to ensure that comparable interest rates apply to IOLTA accounts (Houseman, 2011). To generate additional income for civil legal services, some states have also looked to allocate a portion of court filing fees and fines, as well as to use state abandoned property funds and punitive damages awards (Lang, 2011).

EFFORTS TO CLOSE THE JUSTICE GAP

The fact of the matter is that neither the number of programs nor the resources devoted to these programs are adequate to close the justice gap, and the concept of equal access to justice remains as elusive as ever. As observed by LSC president Jim Sandman during a March 2016 speech at the St. Louis University School of Law, the current civil legal system is "completely inconsistent" with our values (Lippmann, 2016). This recent reflection echoes the sentiment of two leading legal scholars:

> "Equal Justice Under Law" is one of America's most widely embraced and frequently violated legal principles. It appears over countless courthouse doors but by no means describes what goes on behind them. It is a shameful irony that the nation with the world's highest concentration of lawyers does so little to make them accessible to those who need them most. (Rhode & Bam, 2012, p. 3)

Neither the existence of the justice gap, as reflected in statistics recited throughout this chapter, nor efforts to overcome this societal problem are a new phenomenon. The creation of a civil legal services system in this country—however fragmented it may be—was an important first step. It was the creation of this system that allowed the very concept of access to justice to gain traction in the late 1970s (Galanter, 2009). Misperceptions about the availability of counsel in civil cases (as noted above) and growing discontent with the litigious nature of American society, however, precluded the plight of Americans with unmet legal needs from garnering widespread attention (Rhode & Bam, 2012). The landscape began to shift with the formation of statewide bodies to address access to justice issues, a development that paved the way for the justice gap to be defined as a problem in need of workable solutions (Rhode, 2009). As of July 2014, there were access to justice commissions in thirty-two states, the District of Columbia, and Puerto Rico; several other states are currently exploring the possibility of creating such commissions. Most access to justice commissions have been created in the past fifteen years (NCSC, 2014).

Although access to justice commissions and other statewide initiatives were initially concerned primarily with legal aid funding issues, their missions are increasingly encompassing broader access to justice issues, including expanding pro bono and self-help programs, as well as advocating for a right to counsel in civil cases (Houseman, 2011; NCSC, 2014; Zorza, 2009a). As part of examining these issues, access to justice commissions also often address disadvantages created by culture, language, age, and ability (NCSC, 2014). They are an increasingly important means of bringing together different stakeholders (e.g., courts, bar associations, legal aid organizations) to address issues that impact each of them (Houseman, 2011; SRLN, 2008). The prominent role of the highest court in the state is generally viewed as a critical success factor, given the prestige, visibility, and credibility of this institution (NCSC, 2014). The highest court's ability to make the various stakeholders "essential partners" in the access to justice commission is viewed as equally important (NCSC, 2014). The ability of the various stakeholders to work together, however, can be hampered by their differing concerns, which often translates into different research and policy priorities: "To take only the most obvious example, the organized bar has a much stronger economic interest in promoting lawyers' services than in promoting research and policies that support greater reliance on qualified nonlawyers and procedural simplification" (Rhode, 2013, p. 533).

These differences are but one factor contributing to the current lack of consensus within the legal community regarding both the definition of the problem and the viability of the various solutions that have been proposed. To define the problem, it is first necessary to transform the rhetoric of "equal access to justice" into something upon which we can act. However, as described by Rhode (2001, 2013) and Wolf (2012), the vagueness of the term itself can pose problems. For example, does it encompass fair legal processes *and* just outcomes? How much is enough legal assistance? Should legal assistance be available to those who cannot realistically afford attorneys or only to those who are deemed poor by the government? As Rhode (2001) pondered, "[h]ow much claiming and blaming is our society prepared to subsidize?" (p. 1787).

Despite these persistent questions, the access to justice community has coalesced around three main targets for action:

Creation of a Civil Right to Counsel

The establishment of a right to counsel in criminal cases in *Gideon v. Wainwright* is often heralded as evidence of equal access to justice in the United States. The Supreme Court's ruling in *Lassiter*, however, narrowly defined the context in which this principle is recognized. As Robert F. Kennedy once observed, "[w]e have secured the acquittal of an indigent person—but only to abandon him to eviction notices, wage attachments, repossession of goods and termination of welfare benefits" (1965, p. 26). Since that time, we have seen the dialogue surrounding "civil *Gideon*" ebb and flow, as courts have been reluctant to revisit *Lassiter* (Rulli, 2011). In recent years, however, support for the establishment of a civil right to counsel has been growing in tandem with the legal community's increased scrutiny of the justice gap (Engler, 2006, 2010; Gardner, 2006; Lidman, 2006). Increasingly, bar associations and statewide access to justice bodies have voiced their support for an ABA resolution that calls for the provision of counsel, at public expense, to low-income individuals in certain civil cases where basic human needs (e.g., safety, shelter) are at stake (Engler, 2010). "The civil *Gideon* movement moves forward today largely in state and local legislatures, state courts, bar sponsored pilot programs, and in the court of public opinion. Over time, advocates hope that successful outcomes in state and local venues will effectively eliminate the *Lassiter* rule and create a favorable climate for the Supreme Court to reconsider and overrule its holding in *Lassiter*" (Rulli, 2011). There is also a growing recognition that the impacts of providing counsel in civil cases—in terms of financial benefits, judicial efficiency, and improved outcomes—need to be documented (Pollock, 2015).

Development of Different Types of Limited Assistance

This category encompasses services for self-help users through traditional means (e.g., in-person assistance), emerging ICTs (e.g., hotlines, legal information websites), and limited representation (often referred to as unbundled legal services) (Eaton & Holtermann, 2010; Hilbert, 2009; Jennings & Greiner, 2012; Struffolino, 2012; Zorza, 2010). Although assistance for self-help users is the focus of this book, it is important to recognize that between a civil right to counsel and the development of self-help resources lies the concept of limited representation. At the core of this concept is the notion that legal representation does not necessarily need to be an "all or nothing" endeavor. Certain litigants may not need representation at every stage, but "they need to know more than which forms to use, how to docket their cases and what time to appear in court. They need assistance with decision-making and judgment. They need to know their options, possible outcomes and the strategies to pursue their objectives" (ABA, 2014).

Limited representation is typically described as a system in which an attorney offers a selection of services from which a client can choose so that he/she can receive legal assistance with certain aspects of the case (Steinberg, 2011). Underlying the concept of limited representation is the belief that lack of money is a primary reason guiding litigants' decisions to proceed without counsel (Greacen, 2014). "It is the cost of full-service representation in litigation that is prohibitive for many. Many pro se litigants have enough disposable income to pay for the limited representation they need [but] the great majority of lawyers do not offer these potential clients the services they need and can afford. Instead, they present them with an all (full-service) or nothing (wholly self-represented) Hobson's 'choice.' The result is more pro se litigants" (ABA, 2003; see also Eaton & Holtermann, 2010). Limited representation thus represents a middle ground—the litigant retains responsibility for the overall case, while the attorney provides one or more tasks (e.g., legal research, document drafting) for a reasonable fee (Eaton & Holtermann, 2010; Greacen, 2014).

The private bar, by and large, has been reluctant to embrace any form of limited representation out of fear that providing this option will negatively impact their full-service business (ABA, 2003; Greacen, 2014). The ABA, however, has come out in favor of limited-scope representation, as evidenced by Rule 1.2 of the Model Code of Judicial Conduct (the "Model Code") (revised in 2002): "A lawyer may limit the scope of representation if the limitation is reasonable under the circumstances and the client gives informed consent." This support stems from the organization's belief that limited-service clients are most likely to be those who would otherwise proceed as self-represented litigants rather than those who have the means to obtain full-service representation. The ABA has adopted the position that, inasmuch as an expansion of limited representation will lead to a greater number of individuals overall being represented by legal counsel (to some extent or another), it not only expands access to justice but also creates new opportunities for legal professionals (ABA, 2003). The work of the ABA, as well as collaborative efforts among states, has led to consideration of a number of important issues related to limited-scope representation, including requirements for disclosing a lawyer's assistance in preparing documents and procedures for the entry of appearances and withdrawals for attorneys providing limited-scope representation (ABA, 2014).

Closely related to limited representation is the idea of assistance with legal matters by non-attorneys. This has been discussed, for example, within the context of immigration cases. According to Corcoran (2012), 84 percent of individuals appearing in immigration proceedings are unrepresented. There is a growing trend of immigrants seeking assistance from "immigrant consultants" who are, in fact, engaging in the unauthorized practice of law. Advocacy efforts to have courts recognize a constitutional right to counsel in immigration proceedings have failed repeatedly; Corcoran thus advocates for expanded access to duly qualified and trained non-lawyer representatives: "Increasing access to these accredited representatives would provide immigrants with accurate counsel and advice about the availability of immigration relief; reduce backlog and delay in the immigration agencies; and ensure the individual has a competent advocate demanding fair adjudication of his or her application for immigration relief" (p. 645).

Reform within the Judiciary

The emphasis here is on changes that can be made to better equip the courts to address the justice gap. The existence of a relationship between the public's trust and confidence in the court system and the manner in which courts treat litigants proceeding without counsel (often referred to as "self-represented litigants") necessitates a closer examination of the court's interactions with this group of litigants (George & Wang, 2008; Greacen, 2005; Staudt & Hannaford, 2002; Steinberg, 2011; Udell & Diller, 2007; Zorza, 2007). The creation of a court culture that encourages respect for self-represented litigants, encompassing everyone from judges to clerk's office personnel to self-help center staff, is central to this approach (Goldschmidt, 2008; Judicial Council of California, 2007; Zorza, 2004). Judicial buy-in, in particular, is important—judges have the credibility, reputation, and leverage needed to bring about cultural change within a court system (Engler, 2011).

For judges, interacting with self-represented litigants brings to the forefront the challenge of balancing the competing duties of maintaining judicial neutrality and ensuring equal access to justice for all litigants (Berenson, 2001; Engler, 2011; Goldschmidt, 2002; Snukals & Sturtevant, 2007). Rule 2.2 of the Model Code (2011) requires judges to act fairly and impartially. Comment 4 to that rule expressly states that "[i]t is not a violation of this Rule for a judge to make reasonable accommodations to ensure *pro se* litigants the opportunity to have their matters fairly heard."

While there has been a movement among state judiciaries toward adopting language in line with that contained in the Model Code (Engler, 2011), there remains a dearth of clear guidance regarding the parameters of acceptable judicial behavior (Goldschmidt, 2008). In recent years, a number of scholars, including Zorza (2004), Buhai (2009), and Engler (2011), have warned against focusing on the *appearance* of judicial neutrality inasmuch as doing so may discourage judges from providing acceptable assistance to self-represented litigants. Judicial engagement is not the antithesis of judicial neutrality but rather a means to ensure that neutrality is in fact maintained. Zorza and Engler, in particular, advocate for a shift away from the pure adversary model toward the paradigm of judge as "active umpire." Upon adopting that role, judges can then act in a way that minimizes the likelihood of procedural errors depriving the court of relevant evidence and legal arguments (Pearce, 2004).

In addition, others within the court—most notably clerk's office staff—are often forced to make determinations regarding how much assistance to self-represented litigants is appropriate (Johnstone, 2011; Schwarz, 2004). As court personnel, it is permissible for them to give out legal information, but not legal advice—the line between the two, however, is blurry and subject to interpretation (Flaherty, 2002). In an effort to avoid stepping over the line, court personnel may err on the side of giving out the bare minimum of information and, in so doing, place self-represented litigants at an even greater disadvantage (Berenson, 2001; Schwarz, 2004). Furthermore, the extent to which non-judge court personnel are well equipped to assist self-represented litigants is a subject of discussion. While Johnstone (2011) suggests that they are less vulnerable to accusations of breaching impartiality and could lessen the burden on judges by providing more assistance to self-represented litigants, he also raises the question of whether court personnel possess the necessary knowledge, competence, and qualifications to provide a greater level of assistance. Spira (2009) draws attention to other skills that are necessary when working with self-represented litigants, noting that "[c]ourt personnel . . . are not typically trained to deal with 'the anger, fear, frustration, and communication barriers' common to *pro se* litigants" (p. 188).

In the spirit of enhanced judicial engagement, many courts have adopted a bifurcated approach that allows them to focus on the substance (rather than the form) of filings by self-represented litigants. This approach, commonly referred to as the "liberal construction rule," applies "hard" procedural bars (e.g., statutes of limitations, time for filing appeals) but a less rigorous standard of review to the form and content of the documents submitted by self-represented litigants (Albrecht, Greacen, Hough, & Zorza, 2003; Buhai, 2009; Goldschmidt, 2008; Gray, 2007; Landsman, 2009; Schneider, 2011).

In addition to reforms centered on courts' dealings with self-represented litigants, there are also increasing calls for more robust alternative dispute resolution mechanisms (Brodoff, McClellan, & Anderson, 2003; Galanter, 2009). Similarly, there is growing interest in the idea of expanding small claims courts so as to provide a venue where low- and moderate-income individuals could bring claims that otherwise would be economically unfeasible to pursue (Finney & Yanovich, 2006).

While the various initiatives contained within these three broad categories are all worthwhile and deserving of attention from practitioners and scholars, the remainder of this book will focus on neither civil *Gideon* nor reformation of the judiciary but rather on current efforts by legal services providers to work within a deeply troubled system. These efforts are more crucial than ever. In its latest budget request, LSC has asked for an appropriation of $502,700,000, asserting that this figure "represents the funding necessary to restore basic field funding per eligible person to the level of 2007, the last year before the recession began, in inflation-adjusted dollars—$467 million for FY 2017." Even if this budget request is approved, however, LSC will still be working to undo the damage of the latest recession. During that time period, $60 million was slashed from LSC's budget, leading to staff reductions as well as office closures. These supply-side constraints, of course, led to fewer people receiving services from LSC-funded organizations. Moreover, the increased funding LSC received in FY 2015 and 2016 did not fully make up for the drastic budget cuts it experienced during that time period.

As recovery from the recession continues, LSC—and the organizations who rely on it for funding—continue to find themselves in the intractable position of trying to do more with fewer resources. The provision of self-help services through ICTs has been embraced by the legal services community as one way to accomplish this difficult feat. As will be discussed in chapter 2, though, there are many issues that sit squarely at the center of access to information and access to justice that must be considered when providing assistance to self-help users.

NOTES

1. For a comprehensive overview of the current legal services delivery system in the United States (as well as in each of the fifty states and the District of Columbia), see Sandefur and Smyth (2011).

2. IOLTA accounts are pooled, interest-bearing accounts into which attorneys place "nominal or short-term client funds that cannot earn income from the clients. Banks in turn forward the interest earned on these accounts to the state IOLTA program, which uses the money to fund a variety of charitable causes" (ABA, n.d.)

2

Self-Help in the Legal Context

Self-help resources, as touched upon in the last chapter, have been embraced as one option for closing the justice gap. These resources often provide access to information to those who most need it, and the rapid pace of technological developments in recent years has created a multitude of avenues through which this access can be achieved. This chapter will explore who is using self-help resources, as well as the challenges they face in using these resources. It will then conclude with a description of the efforts of courts, legal aid and other community organizations, and libraries to develop self-help resources and programs designed to dismantle these barriers to information access.

GROWTH OF SELF-REPRESENTATION

The upshot of the current legal services system described in chapter 1—and the supply-and-demand imbalance that is the hallmark of this overburdened system—is that many people find themselves navigating the legal system on their own. The steady growth of self-represented litigants since the turn of the twenty-first century has been described by Landsman (2009) as an "inexorably rising tide" (p. 440) and Hilbert (2009) as an "explosion" (p. 547). As early as 2002, commentators were reporting an increase in the number of self-represented litigants in certain areas, such as domestic relations, landlord-tenant, and small claims cases (Johnstone, 2011; Snukals & Sturtevant, 2007; Staudt & Hannaford, 2002; Steinberg, 2011). Numerous sources cite family law cases as the primary generator of the recent growth in self-represented litigants, with well over half of all cases in this area involving one or more such litigants (Berenson, 2001; George & Wang, 2008; Shepard, 2010). Although this increase has been documented through studies conducted by individual court systems (Judicial

Council of California, 2007; Maryland Judiciary, 2007; Massachusetts Supreme Judicial Court, 2008; State of New Hampshire Judicial Branch, 2004) and nationwide surveys of judges (Morris, 2013; Zorza, 2009a), there is limited empirical data on self-represented litigants due to the absence of any nationwide tracking system and the deficient records kept by many states (Glater, 2006; Van Wormer, 2007). This is slowly starting to change, though, as demonstrated by the ongoing Court Statistics Project, funded by the SJI. Through this project, the NCSC and the Conference of State Court Administrators are currently working together to establish a consistent approach to reporting cases with self-represented litigants, with the goal of producing comparable data within and among jurisdictions (SJI, 2014). To date, they have compiled definitions, counting rules, and reporting guidelines for cases involving self-represented litigants.[1] Preliminary data compiled through this project reveals "a wide variation in the percentage of cases with self-represented litigants, underlining the need for more states to report these statistics so that an accurate national picture can be developed" (Schauffler & Strickland, 2015, p. 52).

At the same time, we remain focused on developing a better understanding of the reasons for self-representation. As explained in the previous chapter, self-representation is often not a matter of choice but rather due to financial necessity (Engler, 2011; Smith & Stratford, 2012; Snukals & Sturtevant, 2007; Zorza, 2004). This is true for individuals who may qualify for free legal services as well as for those who are ineligible for such services because of their income level. For middle-income Americans, their failure to qualify for these services does not mean that they have the resources to hire a lawyer (Jefferson, 2013). "The fact is that the majority of Americans live on quite modest incomes and lack the discretionary spending power necessary to purchase expensive legal services in today's market" (Carle, 2001).

Also contributing to the rise in self-representation is a growing perception that lawyers are not always necessary in the pursuit of a legal action. This perception can be traced to two related notions, namely that "the 'Home Depot' do-it-yourself [DIY] method applies to a lot more than house repairs and that in the internet era, the 'noble amateur' can do just about anything as well as the expert" (Landsman, 2009, p. 445). The phenomenon of disintermediation—which obviates the need for "middlemen"—is not unique to the legal field (Greacen, 2011; Judicial Council of California, 2007). Disintermediation in the legal field is closely related to de-professionalization, which refers to social, political, economic, and demographic trends that undermine claims to autonomy, monopoly, and social privilege once enjoyed by well-established professions (Holland, 2013; Rothman, 1984). Traditionally, the monopoly held by duly licensed attorneys was protected by legal sanctions as well as by the reluctance of members of the public to undertake legal tasks for themselves (even when able to do so) or to rely upon non-lawyers for these services.

In recent years, though, the public's perception about what services require the assistance of an attorney has been shifting (Hannaford-Agor & Mott, 2003). Snukals and Sturtevant (2007) and Rothman (1984) both cite a decrease in the "competence gap," due to rising education and literacy levels in the United States, as another factor contributing to the growth of the DIY mentality toward legal proceedings. This belief that some cases are, in fact, simple enough for a layperson to handle is shared by members of the legal profession (Schneider, 2011). At the same time, however, lawyers view the emergence of the DIY mentality in the legal field with a degree of trepidation. Their comprehensive expert knowledge "legitimiz[es] [their] professional prerogatives" (Rothman, 1984, p. 187). If laypersons are capable of doing their work, the extent to which lawyers retain expert authority is called into question.

Driving the processes of disintermediation and de-professionalization in law has been a growth in the amount of legal information to which laypersons now have access, due to the Internet and related ICTs (Berenson, 2001). Members of the public thus are increasingly embracing the notion that access to these resources will enable them to make adequate preparations for their day in court (Berenson, 2001; Hale-Janeke & Blackburn, 2008; Kritzer, 1999; Snukals & Sturtevant, 2007). Statewide legal information websites, which are discussed in depth later in this book, are a prime example of the resources now available to self-represented litigants as a result of technological advancements.

A final contributing factor to the rise in self-representation is an increase in litigiousness (i.e., more people are looking to have their day in court), coupled with a negative perception of lawyers (Snukals & Sturtevant, 2007). According to a 2002 survey conducted by the ABA about the public's perceptions of lawyers, negative attitudes toward lawyers stem from related beliefs that lawyers are "greedy, manipulative, and corrupt"; are too connected to "politics, the judiciary, government, big business, and law enforcement"; and do a "poor job of policing themselves" (Fernandez, 2007). These negative perceptions, in turn, fuel the belief that a lawyer can make a situation worse by decreasing a litigant's sense of control over his or her case. Self-representation then becomes viewed as a self-empowerment tool (Zimerman & Tyler, 2010, p. 499; see also Barclay, 1996). Through this lens, we can begin to see how the Internet and related ICTs, by facilitating access to unprecedented amounts of legal information and fostering a DIY mentality, have contributed to the growth of self-representation in this country.

SELF-REPRESENTED LITIGANTS IN THE LEGAL SYSTEM

The growth of self-representation, however, is not applauded by all. Frequently lodged complaints against self-represented litigants include the following: intake delays in the clerk's office due to incomplete or indecipherable court documents; unfamiliarity with courtroom protocol; overreliance on clerk's office staff for assistance; unrealistic expectations regarding available legal remedies; filing and service of process errors; protracted and/or rescheduled hearings due to self-represented litigants' lack of preparation; and discovery difficulties (Berenson, 2001; George &

Wang, 2008; Greacen, 2005; Hannaford-Agor and Mott, 2003; Henderson, 2003; Rasch, 2011; Spira, 2009).

In some courts, a lingering perception of self-represented litigants as "nuts," "pests," or an "increasing problem," whose very presence creates havoc for the judicial system, persists (Schneider, 2011; Swank, 2004). This remains true despite growing acceptance that a lack of representation generally is not indicative of the merits of a litigant's claims, as well as evidence that self-represented litigants do not actually derail legal processes and courtroom procedures (Greacen, 2014; Schneider, 2011). Even within courts that take a more favorable view of self-represented litigants, however, institutional and administrative requirements create barriers that may be difficult to overcome (Hannaford-Agor & Mott, 2003). The use of unfamiliar legal terminology in pleadings and other documents filed in court, for example, imposes a barrier for many self-represented litigants (Judicial Council of California, 2007).

Underlying these barriers is the fact that, despite the long-standing nature of the right of self-representation, legal and court processes were not designed with self-represented litigants in mind (Zimerman & Tyler, 2010). Many self-represented litigants struggle with reconciling these rules and procedures with the commonsense and social instincts that guide their behaviors and interactions in everyday life (Zimerman & Tyler, 2010). This struggle gives rise to feelings of confusion as self-represented litigants attempt to navigate the complex court system, and later frustration when they feel as though the court is not treating them with the respect to which they are entitled (Henderson, 2003; Rasch, 2011). With no legal writing experience, self-represented litigants' pleadings often contain "emotional language, legal jargon, tangents, and less direct or incomprehensible assertions of fact," while neglecting to include a proper statement of their claims (Schneider, 2011, p. 602). Previous studies have shown that self-represented litigants' preference for stating their claims using language with which they are comfortable (i.e., a narrative approach to tell their story) can result in omissions that adversely impact the disposition of their cases (Goldschmidt, 2008; Schneider, 2011; Spira, 2009; Zimerman & Tyler, 2010).

Giddings and Robertson (2003) assert that effective self-represented litigants demonstrate determination, persistence, a high level of emotional stability, and confidence. However, as observed by Brodoff (2008) and Acosta and Cherry (2008), many self-represented litigants must overcome significant emotional hurdles in order to clearly articulate their claims and prove the necessary facts. Many self-represented litigants thus struggle to demonstrate these qualities. Heightened emotions stem from the circumstances that gave rise to the legal situation, as well as from the anxiety caused by having to find one's way through an often intimidating court environment (Tait, 2011; Widdison, 2013). The trepidation with which laypersons navigate the legal system is starkly different from the dispassionate, informed perspective that guides lawyers' representation of their clients, as well as their interactions with the court and other parties to the case (Pettinato, 2008). As described by Zimerman and Tyler (2010),

> the encounter between lay people and the legal system is challenging for both sides, and pro se litigants are usually perceived as a problem—both to the courts and to themselves. From the litigants' side, there are the obvious difficulties of having to manage within a highly professionalized system whose rules, language and practices they do not know. There is the fear then that pro se litigants' rights and interests are left unprotected. From the courts' side, pro se litigants are considered a burden; the need to deal directly with litigants (rather than professionals) requires modifications in routine processes and court personnel to deviate from their traditional roles and provide additional assistance. (p. 479)

By way of example, it has been reported that individuals with limited English proficiency (LEP) face particularly acute challenges in navigating the legal system (ABA, 2012; Cohen & Weiss, 2009; Rhode, 2004).[2] These challenges exist beyond the individual's intellectual ability to understand the legal issues present in his or her case (Greacen, 2005). Self-represented litigants with LEP are often unable to communicate with court personnel, conduct legal research, read their opponents' legal papers, or understand and participate in court proceedings (Udell & Diller, 2007). In many cases, however, the persistence of these barriers is due not to a lack of awareness but rather to limited resources available for translation services and interpreters (Rhode, 2009; Udell & Diller, 2007). As of the 2010 census, there are approximately twenty-five million LEP individuals living in the United States, representing 9 percent of the population (Migration Policy Institute, 2011; NCSC, 2013). The situation is complicated further by the growing universe of foreign languages found in many American communities: "[i]t is important to note that while some languages are not needed frequently, when the need arises courts must be equipped to provide effective LEP services. This presents challenges when, for example, interpreters for those languages are not available, or forms and instructions are not translated into the particular language" (NCSC, 2013, p. 31).

Language is but one disadvantage that can make the encounter between a layperson and the legal system even more challenging. Self-help users, as noted by Engler (2011) and others, often find themselves in a disadvantaged position due to some combination of socioeconomic status, literacy, education, age, and/or disability. Within the field of information studies, these disadvantages are said to be part of an individual's information environment (Agada, 1999; Davenport, Richey, & Westbrook, 2008; Jones, 2006; Taylor, 1991).

As described by Childers (1975), a person's "'disadvantage' is a function of a particular context, consisting of his immediate physical environment, the social norms that impinge upon his daily activities, the economic and political atmosphere, and his internal makeup—both what they are and what he thinks they are" (p. 8). Groups generally characterized as disadvantaged include the poor, the elderly, the imprisoned, the disabled, the undereducated, the unemployed, and the racially/ethically oppressed. These groups share common characteristics that adversely impact their information environments: they often have low reading literacy and/or low English-language literacy; they are cut off from the popular flows of information in society, creating a closed information universe that is vulnerable to misinformation; their information contacts with society at large tend to be one-way via mass media; and they are less predisposed to view information as a means to alter the undesirable conditions of their lives. Because of these characteristics, they tend not to be active information seekers. This can have a significant impact on their daily lives because, for example, they often do not know about various services that may be available to them (Childers, 1975).

Childers asserts that, while the information needs of the disadvantaged are not fundamentally different from those of the general adult population, they require "large remedial doses of information" (p. 35) in order to be on par with everyone else. Some of the areas in which their information needs are the most acute are housing (e.g., eviction, rent regulation, liability of renters/homeowners, redevelopment issues) and welfare programs (e.g., eligibility requirements, applying for benefits, interrelation among programs, appeals of adverse decisions). All of these issues have legal implications that should not be ignored. Childers, however, identifies three primary barriers that often operate to prevent disadvantaged groups from seeking legal help:

- a tendency not to see a problem as having legal ramifications,
- widespread apathy or downright hostility toward available formal legal services, and
- lack of information.

A recent study by Sandefur (2014) highlights the first point in particular. Finding that people rarely seek assistance from courts or lawyers to address their civil justice situations, she observed that this lack of action is often due to their failure to perceive these situations as legal issues (Sandefur, 2014). The 2002 ABA study on the public's perception of lawyers (Fernandez, 2007), as discussed earlier in this chapter, supports the second proposition. And the third barrier—lack of information—is one that legal self-help services are specifically designed to address.

ADDRESSING THE INFORMATION NEEDS OF SELF-REPRESENTED LITIGANTS

Self-represented litigants struggle primarily because they are laypersons in a system designed for professionals who can operate in that system with ease (Landsman, 2009; Rhode, 2009). Self-help services address this problem head-on by attempting to minimize the unknown. The core of these services is thus the provision of information that aims to level the playing field for all litigants (Brodoff, 2008; Goldschmidt, 2008; Schwarz, 2004). There is general agreement that, in order to engage in effective self-representation, a litigant needs access to information about the relevant substantive law as well as about applicable legal processes and procedures

(Hackerson, 2010; Hale-Janeke & Blackburn, 2008; Pettinato, 2008; Staudt and Hannaford, 2002; Van Wormer, 2007; Wolf, 2012). Both types of information are important, but they serve different purposes. As described by Lawler, Giddings, and Robertson (2012), it is important to distinguish

> between process oriented information which we refer to as "procedural information" the focus of which is on "knowing how" to do something (including knowing what to do and when to do it) and "propositional information" which seeks to explain the relevant substantive law, legal concepts and legal structures and therefore speaks to the "knowing why" to do something within the self-help process. By way of illustration, information which seeks to explain how to fill out a form would, in our characterisation, be a form of "procedural information" while information which explains that a particular tribunal has jurisdiction to hear a type of legal matter would be a form of propositional knowledge in that it increases a person's understanding of why their claim can be dealt with by that tribunal. (p. 207)

Brodoff (2008), in his study of administrative hearings related to Medicaid eligibility, highlighted the centrality of "propositional information" in such legal proceedings. He observed that the relevant body of law is so complex that, even if a self-represented benefit recipient has access to the text of the applicable statutes and relevant case law, he would not be able to decipher it enough to present a cognizable claim. From the beginning, the inherent complexity of the law itself puts a self-represented litigant at a disadvantage vis-à-vis a trained agency representative.

Among the types of procedural information most often sought by self-represented litigants are forms and formal rules of procedure governing court proceedings, such as service of process, preparation of orders, and enforcement of judgments (Berenson, 2001; Henderson, 2003; Hilbert, 2009; Judicial Council of California, 2007; Shepard, 2010; Staudt, 2005; Staudt and Hannaford, 2002). Both forms and rules of procedure, however, run the risk of being rendered incomprehensible by legal jargon. An individual may struggle with finding the form that applies to his situation or with completing the form, particularly in the absence of clear instructions (Berenson, 2001; Owens, 2013). As described by Greacen (2011),

> [t]he form identifies the information needed to request a particular form of legal relief, but does not provide the litigant with the ability to assess whether s/he has adequate grounds to obtain that relief, how to pursue the matter within the court once it has been filed, or how to obtain satisfaction or enforcement of a judgment if one is obtained. In effect, the provision of a form enables a litigant to open the front door to the courthouse, but does not help her or him to decide whether to open that door or, if the door is opened, how to proceed through the courthouse and to exit the court with an enforceable remedy. (p. 9)

Tait (2011) provided a more nuanced characterization of the information needs of self-represented litigants, describing three broad categories of information-related activities in which self-represented litigants typically engage. These three categories encompass both substantive and procedural information that can help self-help users better understand the legal system as well as the specific legal issues they are facing:

- *Informing litigants:* provide orientation and general background information about courts; offer general guidance in navigating the court system.
- *Assessing legal options:* help self-represented litigants understand their specific situation; inform individuals about alternatives to litigation; inform individuals about the implications of proceeding without representation.
- *Pursuing the case:* assist with the process of filing court documents; provide information on follow-up events; assist with resolution and enforcement.

COURTS AND SELF-HELP PROGRAMS

Against the backdrop of this emerging understanding of the information needs of self-represented litigants, courts have taken the lead in developing self-help programs to assist this group of litigants (Goldschmidt, 2002; Schwarz, 2004; Shepard, 2010; Spieler, 2013; Van Wormer, 2007; Zorza, 2009b, 2012a). In assuming this leadership role, courts are acting on a series of recommendations made by the American Judicature Society for them to "study the composition and greatest needs of the self-represented litigants they serve, and design services to effectively meet those needs," "[d]evelop[] programs to assist self-represented litigants [as] a collaborative effort of the bench, court staff, the bar, and the public," and "train court staff on how to assist self-represented litigants" (Henderson, 2003, p. 590).

As early as the mid-1990s, a select number of state courts (e.g., California, Maryland, Michigan) were in the early stages of developing self-represented litigant programs (Downs, 2004). Courts' progress in this area has been rapid, with Spieler (2013) recently noting that (1) almost every state court system now provides some court forms and basic information through its website, and (2) over two-thirds of state court systems provide services to the public, including self-represented litigants, through at least one staffed center located in a courthouse. And, even as courts' budgets have come under fire in recent years, self-represented litigant programs (despite being relatively new) have fared better than other programs, providing some evidence of their perceived value (Zorza, 2009b).

Self-help centers, in which information about court procedures and the law is provided on a one-on-one basis or in workshops, are the backbone of many programs for self-represented litigants.[3] While self-help centers often provide written materials through pamphlets and handouts, and may even house legal reference materials, the focus is generally on the provision of personal assistance (Schwarz, 2004). Although these centers often use volunteer or paid staff attorneys, this assistance does not constitute legal advice or create attorney-client relationships; rather it generally involves answering basic questions and guiding self-represented litigants through the process of completing forms (Fritschel, 2007; SRLN, 2008). Several key best practices have been identified in connection with the operation of self-help centers, including

- availability of computer terminals (Snukals & Sturtevant, 2007);
- use of subject matter-specific self-help materials written in plain English, including explanations of court processes, instructions for filling out forms, and pamphlets that explain how to bring common causes of action and related evidentiary requirements (Clarke & Borys, 2011; Greacen, 2011; Rhode & Bam, 2012; Schwarz, 2004; Snukals & Sturtevant, 2007);
- assistance with completing forms, incorporating the use of online document assembly tools when available (Engler, 2010; Morris, 2013).
- careful consideration of community needs, with particular attention paid to vulnerable populations, including LEP and rural populations (Malcomson & Reid, 2006; Rhode & Bam, 2012; Zorza, 2007); and
- development of rules that clarify the responsibilities of program staff and the scope of services (SRLN, 2008).

Coordination among self-help center staff and judges regarding the type of information that should be provided to self-represented litigants is also viewed as crucial. "If self-help centers and the judges communicate about procedures and the types of facts that judges will take into consideration, handouts can be created and litigants will have been told or informed of many of these things at different times, in different settings, and by different methods. This will reinforce the information and help create consistency so that litigants will know what to expect" (Judicial Council of California, 2007, pp. 6–22). As part of this coordinated effort, judges see to it that self-represented litigants know about available self-help resources (Gray, 2007; Zorza, 2004).

Court-supported self-represented litigant programs are generally viewed as striking an acceptable balance between a court's duty to provide all litigants with meaningful access to justice and its duty of impartiality. As a visible sign of a court's commitment to the ideal of access to justice, these programs work to increase the public's trust in the court system, primarily by demonstrating collaboration among the bench, the bar, and court staff (Berenson, 2001; Engler, 2006; George & Wang, 2008; Goldschmidt, 2002; Greacen, 2005; Henderson, 2003; NCSC, 2012, Zorza, 2010). Moreover, self-help programs take the onus from clerk's staff of having to navigate the gray area between legal advice and legal information (NCSC, 2012), while also minimizing the extent to which judges must "lean over the bench" to level the playing field for SRLs (Engler, 2011; Judicial Council of California, 2007). And, as a practical matter, self-represented litigants who are better informed should be better prepared to litigate their cases, leading to fewer filing and other procedural errors that wreak havoc in the clerk's office and in the courtroom (Albrecht et al., 2003; Flaherty, 2002; NCSC, 2012; SRLN, 2008; Zorza 2009a).

INCREASING COLLABORATION, INCREASING ACCESS TO INFORMATION

A range of professional and community-based organizations (e.g., state bars, legal aid organizations, and libraries) are increasingly working with courts to develop and implement programs for self-represented litigants (Acosta & Cherry, 2008; Cordova, 2010; Lawler et al., 2012; Malcomson & Reid, 2006; NCSC, 2006; SRLN, 2008; Zorza, 2009a, 2010). As community access points, legal aid organizations and libraries, in particular, play an important role. They connect self-represented litigants with the legal information they need by removing barriers created by geography, language, and technology, as well as by providing much-needed emotional support (Mancini, 2013; SRLN, 2008). In recognition of the value of collaborating with librarians to provide self-help services, more state court systems are inviting librarians to serve on their self-help task forces and access to justice bodies (Fritschel, 2007).

Both public libraries and public law libraries are natural partners in the provision of self-help services (NCSC, 2012; Warren, 2004; Zorza, 2010). Public libraries are more likely to be the initial point of contact, but staff may lack the necessary skills and experience to facilitate self-represented litigants' access to legal information (Fritschel, 2007). Public library staff may also be unsure of the parameters of acceptable assistance to self-represented litigants (Zorza, 2010). This stands in contrast to public law library staff's familiarity with operating in a legal environment. They are well versed in the law as well as in tools and resources that can help self-represented litigants understand the law; they understand the process of legal research; they can help users navigate the world of online legal information; they routinely make community service referrals; and they can navigate legal information websites (Houseman, 2001; SRLN, 2008; Warren, 2004). Moreover, law librarians generally have a clear understanding of the distinction between legal advice and legal information (Pettinato, 2008). The expert services available at public law libraries, however, are not always utilized because members of the public are often unaware of their existence.

A July 2014 white paper published by the AALL, as well as an April 2014 report detailing findings from a study conducted by the Law Librarians' Working Group of the SRLN in the summer of 2013, both provide valuable insight into the expanding role of law libraries in the access to justice movement. The SRLN report, in particular, highlighted different ways that law librarians can partner with courts (e.g., by acting as a distribution point for court forms). It also made the important point that the general services provided by law libraries, such as public computers with Internet access and multilingual resources, also support the work of the court. Similarly, AALL's report described several key benefits of housing self-help centers in law libraries:

> The self-help center in the law library . . . benefits from the additional resources and services of expertly trained information staff, computers, print, and online resources, often

> in multiple languages, which can be folded into services provided to the self-help center users, depending upon the user's needs. If someone visits a brief advice clinic held in the law library and the attorney volunteer recommends a certain form to be completed, the user can consult with the librarian about accessing and completing the form in the law library. The packaging of document assembly technologies with a self-help center depicts one of the unique strengths that law libraries contribute to centers located within them. Libraries that are more equipped both on the staffing and resource end can assist even more. Some law libraries provide scanners for patrons who must now e-file documents to the court. (p. 26)

In recognizing that many libraries lack the resources to serve as a full-fledged self-help center, the report describes varying levels of service along a continuum. Other options for libraries to consider include (1) the creation of an educational environment that maximizes available space and offers problem-solving materials, and (2) a collaboration with partners from the legal services community through which the library hosts legal clinics and seminars and develops information packets comprised of forms, instructions, and other resources. Through such collaborative efforts, access to justice partners can circumvent resource constraints while capitalizing on their different organizational strengths to provide an array of information resources and services to self-help users. And, as discussed in the next chapter, the development of websites and other online tools for self-help users offers another opportunity for collaboration among courts, legal aid organizations, and libraries.

EMPIRICAL STUDIES OF LEGAL SELF-HELP SERVICES

Despite generally favorable views of legal self-help services, the extent to which they are effective, that is, the extent to which they actually provide meaningful access to justice, remains an open question (Giddings & Robertson, 2003; Lawler et al., 2012). As observed by Berenson (2001), they are viewed by some as nothing more than a thinly veiled attempt by the legal community to foist off its responsibility for low-income litigants. Underlying this criticism is the notion that turning laymen into lawyers is impossible because there is a "ceiling on lay efficacy" (Hilbert, 2009, p. 6). It is viewed as unrealistic to expect that an individual without legal training can acquire the skills and knowledge one needs in order to "construct[] and present[] a persuasive case consistent with the rules of evidence and focused on the issues critical to making the correct decision" (Johnson, 2009, p. 415).

Much of the research seeking to address these questions has focused on the evaluation of individual programs. Noteworthy examples include Blasi (2004) (evaluation of a California self-help center, using a control group of unassisted litigants); George and Wang (2008) (evaluation of family law courthouse facilitator programs in operation in thirty-five Washington State courts); Spira (2009) (study of settlement assistance program in the U.S. District Court for the Northern District of Illinois); and Smith and Stratford (2012) (case study of brief advice family law clinic in Salt

Lake City, Utah, sponsored by two legal aid programs). The growth of evaluation research has been uneven across the states due to the varying levels of resources that jurisdictions have made available to study self-represented litigant programs.

Early program evaluations typically employed a "survey-based methodology that focused on gathering information on the volume of clients seen by the project, some client demographic information, and a general assessment from the client on whether the program's services were easy to use and were helpful" (Cantrell, 2002, pp. 1582–83). Based on the growing number of individual program evaluations, there is a general sentiment that self-help programs are heavily used and have a positive impact on the legal system as a whole (George & Wang, 2008). Capturing the perspectives of self-represented users, however, is notoriously difficult, as discussed by Cantrell (2002), Engler (2010), George and Wang (2008), Lawler et al. (2012), and Smith and Stratford (2012). They are a hard to reach group for several reasons, including their reluctance to talk about personal legal issues and the reality that many never actually make their way into the legal system; they may, for example, be deterred from filing suit because they cannot figure out how to fill out the required forms.

Thus, most data collected from self-represented litigants to date has focused on their satisfaction with the services they received (Cantrell, 2002; Engler, 2010; Rhode, 2013; Rhode & Bam, 2012; Selbin et al., 2012; Smith & Stratford, 2012), with studies typically finding high levels of client satisfaction (Engler, 2010; Rhode, 2009). Client satisfaction data provides some valuable information about the experiences of self-represented litigants inasmuch as "satisfaction matters because a wealth of psychological research makes clear that people's subjective perceptions of how their concerns were represented affects the legitimacy of the legal process" (Rhode, 2013, p. 536). Moreover, low levels of satisfaction can help providers identify when and for whom self-help resources are not adequate (Smith & Stratford, 2012).

There are numerous limitations to client satisfaction data, however, as noted by Cantrell (2002), Selbin et al. (2012), and Rhode (2013). The high levels of satisfaction may have more to do with self-help users' sense of relief from having received some assistance rather than with the actual impact of this assistance (often referred to as a "halo effect") (Cantrell, 2002). Smith and Stratford's study of a brief advice clinic (2012) demonstrates the aftermath of the halo effect. While 84.8 percent of users who received a form reported a high level of satisfaction, a substantial decline in this initial satisfaction was noted during the follow-up period after users had actually attempted to complete the forms.

Due to the focus on client satisfaction data, little is currently known about under what circumstances and for whom self-help resources and services are most useful (Lawler, Giddings, & Robertson, 2009, 2012). In other words, our current understanding of self-help users' information needs is quite limited. There is some evidence that people with a legal information need are likely to turn to other people for assistance before consulting written materials (Hunter, Banks, & Giddings, 2009; Scott, 2000). But, as to self-represented litigants who look beyond their friends and family for legal information assistance, we know little about whether they are able to make effective use of self-help materials (Bruce, 2000; Malcomson & Reid, 2006; Scott, 2000; Spieler, 2013).

Comprehensive studies undertaken in Canada (MacFarlane, 2013) and Australia (Lawler et al., 2012), however, demonstrate the feasibility of gathering more nuanced data about the experience of being a self-represented litigant. The latter—a three-year exploratory study of self-help legal resources and practices within Australia—focused on the extent to which there is a match between the information being provided through self-help resources and the articulated needs of self-helpers. The central research question explored in this study involved

> whether, at a point of legal exigency, the needs of individual users for basic *process oriented* and *solutions focused* self-help resources (a common recurring need expressed by self-helpers throughout each of the four case studies we explored) conflict with and potentially undermine the importance providers attach to imparting sufficient legal knowledge, information and skills to allow the user to work through the required legal processes as an "informed citizen." (p. 186)

Key findings from this study include the following:

1. Resources targeted at helping individuals at a "point of legal exigency" (e.g., individuals experiencing a current legal problem) differ markedly from community legal education resources that seek to increase awareness about legal rights and processes in a more general manner.
2. Self-helpers want information geared specifically toward helping them with their current problem and are not interested in engaging with the legal system in a way that will have a broader impact on their lives (i.e., users are not seeking empowerment or transformation through self-help).
3. Self-helpers assess the utility of a resource based on how closely it matches their motivations for undertaking self-help (i.e., does it provide easy access to the legal system?).
4. Self-helpers are more interested in learning about how to navigate legal processes and less concerned with information that explains the relevant substantive law.

Based on these findings, the authors recommended that providers involve users in the development of self-help resources so that they are not solely reflecting the "provider's perspective of what a layperson would need to navigate the legal system" (p. 219).

This discussion of previous research focused on legal self-help services highlights an important issue, namely, the need to develop a clearer understanding of how legal self-help services are designed and implemented. The proliferation of technology-enabled legal self-help services—the subject of chapter 3—elevates the importance of this issue as these services potentially create new barriers to information access.

NOTES

1. Information about this component of the Court Statistics Project is available at http://www.courtstatistics.org/Other-Pages/SRL_Main.aspx.

2. The federal government defines LEP individuals as those "who do not speak English as their primary language and who have a limited ability to read, speak, write, or understand English" (LEP.gov, n.d.).

3. In August 2014, the ABA's Standing Committee on the Delivery of Legal Services released a report in connection with a nationwide survey of self-help centers, detailing variations among states in terms of staffing (including volunteers), funding sources, languages offered, the use of e-filing, service methods, substantive areas of law in which services are provided, and volume of clients served.

3

The Expanding Role of Technology in Legal Self-Help

The Washington State Supreme Court's adoption of the Access to Justice Technology Principles, which were developed by the state Access to Justice Board in 2004, was one of the earliest statements to crystallize the intersection of access to information, justice, and technology. These principles brought to light the growing awareness among members of the access to justice community that technology is to be deployed in a way that neither creates nor increases barriers to equal access to justice. The importance of considering access issues has only become clearer in the intervening years, as websites operated by courts and providers of legal services now function as primary mechanisms for delivering information to self-help users about their legal rights, as well as about legal processes, courtroom procedures, and appropriate forms (Greacen & Jones, 2013; Morris, 2013).

These websites, and the interactive tools and features that are increasingly being built into them, are an outgrowth of the "traditional" court-based, in-person services discussed in the previous chapter. Both types of programs generally share the same goals (i.e., the provision of information, not advice) and thus must remain attuned to the information needs of self-help users. The literature also reveals that, as with traditional services, collaboration among courts, legal services providers, and other community organizations often underlies technology-based initiatives (Acosta & Cherry, 2008; SRLN, 2008). Traditional self-help programs and technology-based self-help services contend with similar struggles as well. Both must find a way to balance institutional goals and client needs, which may not always be aligned well (Hunter et al., 2009; Lawler et al., 2009; Van Wormer, 2007). Collaborating organizations in both contexts must often work through the general problems of staff resistance and skepticism, funding, and training (Herman, 2007).

The use of Internet-based materials clearly has advantages over print materials to the extent that they are less expensive to produce, as well as more efficient to disseminate and update (Giddings & Robertson, 2003; Ledray, 2013; Scott, 2000). Several other key advantages to providing information to self-help users via technological means have been noted: (1) concerns regarding the gray area between legal advice and legal information are minimized (Van Wormer, 2007); (2) information is made available to a wider audience (Scott, 2000); and (3) content from courts, legal services providers, and other sources is more easily integrated together (Ledray, 2013). But, as noted by Smith (2013), "[d]elivery systems are only a means to an end. There is no escaping the fact that the best websites . . . have the best advice both in terms of . . . substantive content and practicality. This is absolutely crucial and is an expression of the 'gold in; gold out: rubbish in; rubbish out' principle" (p. 2).

The potential of technology-based services to reach a greater number of self-help users, in particular, has appealed to many who are fighting to close the justice gap. The word "potential" is of utmost importance here. The existence of the technology underlying the websites, in and of itself, cannot and will not close the justice gap. In using the technology, care should be taken to address the known barriers to information access with which many self-help users must contend (Cabral et al., 2012; Hilbert, 2009; Lawler et al., 2012; Ledray, 2013; Owens, 2013; Rhode, 2009; Staudt & Hannaford, 2002; Van Wormer, 2007). As noted by Zorza and Horowitz (2006), the delivery of legal information through ICTs requires

> a capacity to access the system that some do not have—whether the capacity is financial, educational, technological, physical or mental, or geographical. When these access limitations outweigh the benefits of the technology, it defeats the goal of creating greater access to courts through the use of technology. (p. 249)

Early on, the very existence of barriers created by such "access limitations" led to some resistance about shifting money away from traditional legal services, reflecting a common sentiment that low-income individuals require face-to-face assistance and paper-based approaches (Ledray, 2013). The barriers to information are both longstanding and deeply entrenched, operating to impede access to online legal information by those with the greatest need. While these barriers are not insurmountable, it is necessary to have a clear idea of both the nature and scope of these barriers in order to address them.

IDENTIFYING BARRIERS TO INFORMATION ACCESS

What then are the barriers that prevent technology-based self-help services from being usable by and useful for self-help users? Any discussion of information barriers and disadvantages should begin with an acknowledgement of the digital divide, originally defined by the National Telecommunications and Information Administration as "the divide between those with access to new technologies and those without." Factors such as socio-economic status, education level, language, disability, age, and geography are said to contribute to the persistence of this divide (Freedman & Henderson, 2008; Gordon, 2001; Helbig, Gil-Garcia, & Ferro, 2009; Horrigan, 2010; Jaeger, Bertot, Thompson, Katz, & DeCoster, 2012; Pettigrew, Durrance, & Unruh, 2002; Robinson, DiMaggio, & Hargittai, 2003; Van Wormer, 2007; Wolf, 2012; Yu, 2011).

Given the widespread perception that the Internet is everywhere, lack of Internet access is not generally viewed as a significant barrier to most people living in the United States (Wolf, 2012). Such access, however, is not universal (Van Wormer, 2007). In June 2015, the Pew Research Center issued a report that examined trends in Internet access in the United States between 2000 and 2015 (Perrin & Duggan, 2015). During that fifteen-year period, the percentage of American adults using the Internet increased from 52 to 84 percent. More significantly, the report confirmed varying levels of Internet access among different groups: "For some groups, especially younger adults, those with high levels of education and those in more affluent households, internet is at full penetration. For other groups, such as older adults, those with less educational attainment, and those living in lower-income households, adoption has historically been lower but rising steadily. . . . At the same time digital gaps exist." Several of these remaining gaps are particularly relevant when thinking about technology-based legal services, given Engler's finding that self-help users are often disadvantaged due to a combination of socio-economic status, education, age, and/or other factors (2011):

- 96 percent of young adults use the Internet, whereas only 58 percent of adults aged sixty-five and older do so.
- 95 percent of adults with college or graduate degrees use the Internet, whereas only 66 percent of adults who have not completed high school do so.
- 97 percent of adults living in households with an annual income of at least $75,000 use the Internet, whereas only 74 percent of adults living in households with an annual income under $30,000 do so.

It is also important to note that not all access is created equal. Broadband is high-speed Internet access, currently defined by the Federal Communications Commission (FCC) as a minimum download speed of 25 Mbps and a minimum upload speed of 3 Mbps. The rate of broadband adoption is somewhat lower than that for the Internet in general and has remained slow since 2009 (Horrigan, 2012). Per data released by the National Telecommunications and Information Administration (NTIA) in May 2013, broadband is available at 98 percent of U.S. households (NTIA, 2013b), but only 72 percent of these households have adopted broadband (NTIA, 2013a). As with the Internet in general, broadband adoption is rather uneven, with individuals living in households with incomes under $20,000, older adults, and individuals with less than a high school diploma being significantly less likely to have a broadband subscription as compared to wealthier, younger, and/or more educated individuals (Tomer and Kane, 2015). While the price of monthly subscriptions for broadband "is the most obvious barrier . . . [c]ommunities with a large percentage of non-adopters face multiple overlapping challenges to broadband use, from skill and language barriers to problems with providers to overburdened community intermediaries and overstretched public Internet access points" (Dailey, Bryne, Powell, Karaganis, & Chung, 2010). Lack of broadband access has particular significance in the context of connecting self-help users with the information they need, as broadband is essential to support many of the advanced technologies that help disadvantaged individuals overcome information barriers. These include video streaming (for those with limited literacy) and video conferencing (for those unable to obtain in-person services due to disability, lack of transportation, or lack of child care) (Gordon, 2001).

Internet access and adoption trends show that many gaps are steadily (albeit sometimes slowly) decreasing. However, even if universal broadband access was achieved, the fact that self-help users possess the technological means to access online legal information does not necessarily mean that they can and will do so. The digital divide thus is not simply about access to the Internet (Bertot, 2003; Gordon, 2001). As aptly noted by Gordon (2001), "[t]he reality . . . is that the digital divide . . . is actually an information-age iteration of myriad economic and social inequities of opportunity and outcome that demands our attention as much as more familiar inequities related to income, employment, housing, health care, [and] race" (p. 46). Access to this information is equally dependent on a range of literacy skills, and users facing limitations with respect to one or more of these skills are likely to face an uphill battle. Scott (2000), in an early discussion of online legal information, noted that

> [i]nformation is a step along the way, not a product. People want their problem solved, they do not want a piece of information. It is not enough to simply provide web sites with legal information on them, no matter how well the information is packaged. Information is only of value if it is found, used and understood. (p. 28)

Each of the following literacy skills is key to an individual being able to find, use, and understand online legal information in this country:

Basic Literacy

In 2011, Sandefur and Smyth observed that "[w]hile most Americans are functionally literate in English, illiteracy rates range widely across states, from a low of 6% of state populations lacking basic prose literacy in English to a high of 23%. An average of 11.7% of state populations lack basic prose literacy skills in English" (p. 15). According to the National Center for Education Statistics (n.d.), those who lack basic prose literacy may not be able to read or understand any written information or may only be able "to locate easily identifiable information in short, commonplace prose text in English, but nothing more advanced." Although websites are increasingly incorporating multimedia components, much of the information presented via this medium is written. The ability to use online information then is often dependent on a user's basic literacy (Gordon, 2001).

English-Language Literacy

For LEP individuals, the very fact that legal information is presented in the English language can pose a significant barrier. As will be discussed in subsequent chapters, a growing number of legal services providers have been addressing the problem of language access, and so the extent to which current online legal self-help services are accessible by LEP individuals varies widely. Data is available, however, to inform decisions about the most pressing linguistic needs. For example, according to the Migration Policy Institute (2011), the top five languages spoken by LEP individuals in the United States are Spanish, Chinese, Vietnamese, Korean, and Tagalog. An additional issue to consider when thinking about language access, however, is the increasing language diversity in certain parts of the country. The question becomes whether it is practical—or even possible—to endeavor to meet everyone's needs. There are a number of foreign language translation tools available, but legal service providers are generally in the early stages of evaluating the relative strengths and weaknesses of these tools (Hogue & Hineline, 2013).

Legal Information Literacy

In the context of providing legal information, an important consideration is how understandable it is by individuals with little familiarity and understanding of the law (Abel, 2012; Hunter et al., 2009; Ledray, 2013; Pettinato, 2008; Tait, 2011). After all, as observed by Scott (2000), the value of information in this context lies in its ability to help people solve a problem. It may be difficult, however, for providers of online legal information and services to put themselves in the position of self-help users:

> The inherent bias of legally trained professionals is towards the use of familiar and precise legal terminology because specific legal terms are used in statutes and case law and have acquired an accretion of accepted meaning and nuance that seems difficult or impossible to convey in a few words of plain English. The legally trained mind seems invariably to favor precision in legal meaning over general understandability when choosing the words to use in a form. (Greacen, 2011, p. 23)

The problem is amplified by the fact that self-help users who are novices with respect to legal information may process any information they read differently and thus are more likely to experience information overload. This is due, at least in part, to their inability to sort through the information and determine what is relevant and important to their pursuits (Tait, 2011). Moreover, written documents do not present an opportunity to obtain clarification if the reader is confused (Maryland Access to Justice Commission, 2012). And without adequate clarification, a self-help user may not know what action is expected or required of him. A failure to act when action is required, unfortunately, can potentially lead to an adverse outcome in the justice system (Cohen & Weiss, 2009).

Digital Literacy

Not all individuals who have access to the Internet possess the skills needed to use the technology, locate and retrieve useful information, evaluate the relevance of the information, and apply the information to the problem at hand (Bertot, 2003; Thompson, Jaeger, Taylor, Subramaniam, & Bertot, 2014). A 2013 Pew report that examined Internet usage and non-usage revealed that lack of access to the Internet was not the most frequently cited reason for non-use (Zickuhr, 2013). Only 7 percent of survey respondents gave that reason, compared to 34 percent citing lack of relevance and 32 percent citing difficulty of use. The concept of digital literacy, which dates to the 1990s, was originally viewed as synonymous with the Internet, networking, and computers in general. More recently, the concept has been subsumed within the notion of twenty-first-century literacy, an overarching term that weaves together the threads of technology literacy, information literacy, media creativity, and social competence and responsibility (Adeyemon, 2009). As explained in the National Broadband Plan (FCC, 2010),

> Though there is no standard definition, digital literacy generally refers to a variety of skills associated with using ICT to find, evaluate, create and communicate information. It is the sum of the technical skills and cognitive skills people employ to use computers to retrieve information, interpret what they find and judge the quality of that information. (p. 90)

Librarians are increasingly playing an important role in helping individuals develop their digital literacy skills (Jaeger, Gorham, Bertot, & Sarin, 2014; Zorza, 2012b). This reflects a broader phenomenon that has emerged, as the barriers that many self-help users face due to limited literacy skills in any of the areas outlined above render it difficult—if not impossible—for them to use online self-help resources without some level of assistance. Their first instinct may not be to search for the information online but rather to seek face-to-face assistance from librarians, court staff, social services providers, and others. The providers of in-person assistance and education therefore function as information intermediaries and become instrumental in connecting self-help users with online legal information (Dailey et al., 2010; Gordon, 2001; Scott, 2000). "Users' ability to assimilate information . . . depends upon their level of existing knowledge; thus, the prior provision of face-to-face advice can build a platform for greater understanding and more effective use of written information" (Hunter et al., 2009, p. 16). As will be discussed in chapter 6, we are seeing an increasing number of collaborations among courts, legal services organizations, and other community organizations that make effective use of information intermediaries.

UNDERSTANDING BARRIERS TO INFORMATION ACCESS

Thinking about the hurdles that many self-help users must face in accessing online legal information and services, the crux of the problem lying at the intersection of access to information, technology, and justice begins to emerge—as we will explore in chapters 4 and 5, we now know that an abundance of time, energy, and resources are being devoted to the development and maintenance of online resources and services for self-help users. The supply-and-demand problem plaguing the civil legal services delivery system in this country clearly establishes the need for these resources and services. But, their mere existence does not necessarily mean that we are adequately addressing the barriers to information access created by limited literacy skills. Put another way, we do not know if users are in fact able to use the information that is ostensibly created for their benefit.

Unfortunately, there is limited empirical research focused on technology-based legal self-help services to aid us in answering this question. In 2000, Bruce observed that "electronic legal information spaces are arenas for interactions about which we know little—interactions between the public and black-letter law" (p. 31). To a large extent, this remains true today. Studies in Canada (Birnbaum & Bala, 2012; MacFarlane, 2013) have explored the use of online legal resources by self-represented litigants, and Smith (2013) examined the innovative approaches adopted by legal services communities in several countries (e.g., the Netherlands, Wales) in the delivery of legal information to the public. In the United States, empirical research has explored the identification of barriers that users commonly face in accessing online legal information (e.g., Smith & Stratford, 2012).

What has not been studied in depth, however, is the extent to which these barriers have been considered and addressed during the development and implementation of online legal information and services. Research in the related area of e-government[1] offers a good starting point for the examination of this particular issue. Notably, e-government research in recent years has become increasingly focused on understanding barriers to information access from the perspective of users (de Róiste, 2013; Gauld, Goldfinch, & Horsburgh, 2010; Pietersen, Ebbers, & van Dijk, 2007; Reddick, 2005). These studies reflect awareness that increased efficiency should not be the only goal when providing online services (Bertot & Jaeger, 2006, 2008; Davenport et al., 2008). They also reflect a growing understanding that e-government use depends on more than physical access to ICTs—factors such as users' motivations and digital literacy skills must also be considered (Pietersen et al., 2007; Slack & Rowley, 2004; Verdegem & Verleye, 2009). As a first step, Verdegem and Verleye (2009) believe it is important to consider the different phases through which an e-government user must pass when acquiring new information:

- becoming aware of the service,
- determining its perceived utility (factoring in both usefulness and ease of use),
- attempting to gain access to the service,

- attempting to use the service to fulfill his or her need, and
- evaluating the extent to which he or she is satisfied with the service.

A careful assessment of how users fare at each phase is central to a user-centered approach to e-government. One often-repeated criticism, however, is that service providers typically fail to assess the information needs of their target users prior to launching an e-government website or service, creating a situation in which the service provided does not match users' perceptions of what is actually needed (Slack & Rowley, 2004; Verdegem & Verleye, 2009). To address this situation, it has been suggested that government agencies include user assessments in their evaluation efforts to develop a clearer profile of their users and then use this enhanced understanding to guide website development (de Róiste, 2013). Users, for example, can provide relevant insight into how they seek and acquire information, as well as how they solicit expertise (Bertot & Jaeger, 2008).

ADDRESSING BARRIERS TO INFORMATION ACCESS

While more empirical research focused on online legal information and services is clearly needed, scholars and practitioners alike have made great strides in terms of developing best practices regarding the provision of information to self-help users via the Internet (Berkman Center, 2010; Greacen, 2011; SRLN, 2008; Van Wormer, 2007). These best practices have proven to be rather valuable, as they highlight the ways that website developers can address the full range of barriers to information access.

Early in the development of online legal information, Bruce (2000) identified the importance of designing websites with the needs of users in mind. The best practices that have emerged since that time align well with the e-government research discussed above, as they coalesce around the idea that user needs should be reflected in both the content made available through a legal information website and the design of the site.

Website Content

To be useful to self-help users, information must be accurate and relevant (Smith, 2013; Van Wormer, 2007). Decisions regarding the type of content to include must reflect an understanding that, in many cases, self-help users need basic information about the legal system and court proceedings above all else (Hopwood, 2011). Van Wormer (2007) compiled a list of information resources that should be available on court websites. Many of the items on the list apply equally to websites maintained by legal services organizations and their collaborators, including

- access to court rules and forms,
- a directory of free and low-cost legal service providers,

- links to relevant substantive laws of the jurisdiction, and
- general information on areas of substantive law most relevant to self-help users.

To ensure the integrity of the website, content should be reviewed and updated on a regular basis (Berkman Center, 2010; Widdison, 2013).

In addition to the content itself, consideration needs to be given to presenting the content in a way that meshes with how self-help users view legal issues (Barclay, 1996; Berkman Center, 2010). In order to be digestible by self-help users, the information should be structured in a way that walks them through the process of solving the problem that brought them to the website in the first place:

> It is becoming widely accepted that legal guidance needs to be orientated towards "life episodes" rather than traditional legal categories. . . . These are important first steps, but much more is needed. While guidance has to be as simple as possible, it should be no simpler. So, guidance should integrate as much knowledge and know-how as is necessary in a practical, step-by-step approach to enable self-helpers to solve their legal problems. (Widdison, 2013, p. 3)

The step-by-step approach, for example, can be accomplished online through the use of hypertext links that also work to prevent users from being overwhelmed by too much information at any one time (Greacen, 2011). This approach can also incorporate a continuum of resources to better serve the needs of users with varying levels of understanding, from plain-language materials to more sophisticated resources (Greacen, 2011; Scott, 2000).

Moreover, the use of plain language, whenever possible, is strongly recommended when developing written materials for self-help users in both print and online formats. A primary focus of the plain-language movement is clear communication that takes into account who one's users are in order to better help them find, use, and understand the information they need (Plain Language Action and Information Network, 2011). Plain-language court forms, in particular, are growing in popularity (Rosenberg, 2016). In 2005, Mindlin conducted a quantitative study to build upon anecdotal evidence that plain-language court forms are more readable and more likely to be read.[2] Finding a statistically significant difference in readability and reading interest as measured by readers' perceptions of the level of difficulty of the forms, Mindlin concluded that the treated, plain-language forms were easier to understand and more completely understood by readers. In addition, Mindlin suggested that the use of plain-language forms will benefit the court as well—self-represented litigants' greater understanding of the forms will lead to greater compliance (thereby easing burdens on judges and the clerk's office to rectify litigants' errors). Moreover, as observed by Dyer et al. (2013), the use of plain-language forms enhances the legal system's ability to serve LEP individuals: "It has also been shown [by Mindlin] that interpreter services can be conducted with [40 percent] less expense when translating plain-language forms, as compared to other forms" (pp. 1086–87).

While there are no specific standards governing the readability of forms and other legal materials, online guidance is available at http://plainlanguage.gov and http://www.writeclearly.org (Greacen, 2011; Maryland Access to Justice Commission, 2012). Different opinions have been expressed with respect to the appropriate reading level to target when writing for self-help users, with Greacen (2011) advocating for forms to be written at a third-grade level and the Maryland Access to Justice Commission (2012) suggesting that an eighth-grade level is acceptable given the inherent complexity of legal language. To ensure that an appropriate reading level is being used, Cantrell (2002) recommended conducting readability evaluations so as to provide "some assurance at the outset that a potential client will be comfortable with the materials. Then, clients can be interviewed after they receive or use materials as a double check evaluation on the accessibility of the materials" (pp. 1586–87). According to Dyer et al. (2013), twenty-four states currently have extensive plain-language court forms for use in family law and other cases, with fourteen of these states mandating the use of such forms.

Each of the following suggested practices identified in the literature can increase the readability of written legal information, regardless of format:

- use of familiar words and phrases, rather than foreign, archaic, and noun-heavy phrases (Dyer et al., 2013; Mindlin, 2005) (e.g., "divorce" rather than "dissolution"; "obey" rather than "comply with"; "rules" rather than "provisions");
- use of active voice and direct address (Dyer et al., 2013);
- explanation of specialized terms (Maryland Access to Justice Commission, 2012; Mindlin, 2005);
- use of readability tools to check reading level (Maryland Access to Justice Commission, 2012); and
- incorporation of visual aids to improve readability of layout (Gordon, 2001; Maryland Access to Justice Commission, 2012).

Furthermore, the potential of technology-based self-help services to address concerns regarding the readability of legal information should be maximized. As explained by Smith (2013), these services should involve more than putting print pamphlets online but rather should harness the power of ICTs to combine text, graphics, and multimedia elements to make information more digestible. Similarly, Widdison (2013) offers the following discussion of the incorporation of non-textual elements:

> For the substantial proportion of the population with limited literacy skills, sole reliance on text is a major additional barrier. In a multimedia digital environment such as the Internet, purely textual representation is entirely unnecessary. . . . Appropriate use of graphics in the form of diagrams and flowcharts can greatly improve the understanding of accompanying text. Images in the form of photographs and illustrations not only support text, they can sometimes substitute for it e.g. with a "comic-book" format. Sound bites may sometimes have a useful role to play. Best of all, surely, are video clips that e.g.

provide short lectures in lay terms on relevant issues, or show other self-helpers going through the various stages of a problem solving strategy. (p. 4)

Even with plain-language content, users may still struggle with understanding the available information due to the inherent complexity of law or to language barriers. Legal information websites, however, do not need to be stand-alone resources. They can link users to additional sources of support and information through phone and/ or chat services so that frustrated users do not abandon their pursuits (Ledray, 2013; Smith, 2013). In addition, multilingual content should be included to whatever extent possible (Berkman Center, 2010; Birnbaum & Bala, 2012).

Website Design

The process of website design should be a collaborative effort, at the very least involving the input of both users and providers of legal services (Scott, 2000; Smith, 2013). Herman (2007) suggests that data can be collected about user needs and preferences in a variety of ways:

> An accurate assessment of what the user really needs from your Web site, knowing what the user cares about the most, using the right words, and a less-is-more approach to Web site design will increase the chances that your Web site will meet the exact needs of your user. Utilizing caseload statistics and information from court staff to pinpoint the greatest need provides a starting point for developing on-point Web content. Data on user needs can also be gathered through surveys, focus groups, or an online user-feedback tool. Involving court staff, community stakeholders, and the self-represented themselves in the development of content will help to ensure useful Web sites that will meet the ongoing information needs of this audience. (p. 30)

The design process should also involve consideration of accessibility issues (e.g., compatibility with assistive technologies) so that individuals with disabilities have effective access to information on the website (Berkman Center, 2010; Birnbaum & Bala, 2012).

Increasingly, the rise of mobile technology has implications for website design. Per data released by the Pew Research Center in April 2015, 90 percent of American adults own a cell phone and 64 percent own smartphones (Smith, 2015). Further, certain demographic groups who have traditionally found themselves on the wrong side of the digital divide—young adults, minorities, those with no college experience, and those with lower household income levels—are more likely to be "smartphone dependent" (i.e., lack any other type of high-speed access at home or have limited options for going online other than their cell phone) (Smith, 2015). A 2016 study conducted by Urban Insight found that nearly half (46 percent) of traffic to legal services websites came through smartphones and tablets. Furthermore, increases in web traffic are attributed primarily to mobile device users, while traffic from desktop users remains more or less static. The prevalence of mobile devices thus mandates consideration of how to expand current technology-enabled self-help services to incorporate both texting and mobile applications (Ledray, 2013). In response to this shift, legal services websites are gradually adopting responsive design, with the percentage of websites doing so increasing from 26 percent in 2014 to 42 percent in 2015 (Urban Insight, 2016). Accordingly, increasing consideration is also being given to how the presentation of content needs to evolve. For example, the use of bulleted lists, fewer words, and short paragraphs is of even greater importance now, as both reading and comprehension are more difficult on a mobile device (Cabral et al., 2012).

Looking across the various best practices identified in the literature, it becomes clear that a primary consideration is how to package the information in a way that the target audience will understand and be able to use effectively (Bruce, 2000; Clarke & Borys, 2011; Scott, 2000). Notwithstanding the development and publication of sound best practices, however, the extent to which website developers have created legal information websites that are useful for and usable by those with the greatest need remains an open question: "[I]t appears that the most comprehensive *pro se*-oriented websites are designed for the edification of lawyers and the judicial community, not for [self-represented litigants] themselves" (Van Wormer, 2007, p. 1008). We are thus left to ponder whether these best practices have, in fact, been implemented by providers of legal services as well as others in the access to justice community. And that is one of the principal questions underlying the research presented in chapters 4 and 5. This research, conducted during my doctoral studies, was designed to open the "black box" of one specific group of technology-based legal self-help services—statewide legal information websites—in an effort to better understand how individuals involved in the development and implementation of these websites have attempted to address known barriers to information access.

NOTES

1. E-government refers to the use of information technologies by government to improve and build relationships with citizens, businesses, and other arms of government (World Bank, n.d.).

2. Although Mindlin's study did not focus on online materials, her findings are relevant here in light of the increasing number of states that are incorporating document assembly functions into their statewide legal information websites.

4

Overview of Statewide Legal Information Websites

Situated squarely at the nexus of access to information, technology, and justice is a collection of websites that have been developed to help those who have fallen into the justice gap, struggling to navigate an unfamiliar and complex legal system. The network of statewide legal information websites that spans the fifty states, the District of Columbia, and several U.S. territories can be traced to LSC's Technology Initiative Grant (TIG) program (Aaron, 2012; Cabral et al., 2012; Hornsby, 2010; Morris, 2013; Owens, 2013; Snukals & Sturtevant, 2007; Staudt, 2005, 2009; Zorza, 2012b). Appendix A provides a list of current statewide legal information websites in the United States.

The TIG program funds projects that use technology to:

1. effectively and efficiently provide high quality legal assistance to low-income persons and to promote access to the judicial system through legal information, advice, and representation;
2. improve service delivery, quality of legal work, and management and administration of grantees; and
3. develop, test, and replicate innovative strategies that can enable grantees and state justice communities to improve clients' access to high-quality legal assistance through an integrated and well-managed technology system (LSC, n.d., "Technology Initiative Grant Program").

Only organizations that are current recipients of LSC basic field grants are eligible to apply for TIGs[1]; other organizations can participate as project partners. Since its inception in 2000, 640 grants totaling more than $53 million have been awarded through the TIG program. TIG funding has fluctuated over the years, ranging from a high of $7 million in 2001 to a low of $1.2 million in 2006 (Staudt, 2009). Funding in recent years has been relatively steady. Between 2011 and 2014, TIG program funding stayed in the range of $3.2–$3.4 million (LSC, n.d., "LSC Funding"). In 2015, the TIG program budget increased to $4 million.

Early on, the TIG program was instrumental in helping legal aid organizations develop websites intended for use by the public. Over the span of four years, states were eligible to receive $100,000 for the development of a statewide website so long as they used one of two LSC-supported templates, Pro Bono Net or Kaivo Software (Melton, Snider, & Zorza, 2005).

Pro Bono Net is a national non-profit organization that partners with non-profit legal organizations throughout the United States and Canada to increase access to justice for poor and moderate-income individuals. Statewide legal information websites that use the LawHelp template are hosted by Pro Bono Net, enabling states to focus on content development and management rather than on software and hardware issues. The template complies with Section 508 of the Rehabilitation Act Amendments of 1998 and has undergone extensive usability testing. The LawHelp template is flexible and customizable, providing for the incorporation of document assembly functions, multimedia materials, and XML. As noted in a 2007 report, however, there are limits to its customizability as "all changes to the platform must flow through Pro Bono Net and will affect all users collectively" (Weber, 2007, p. 8). As of July 2016, twenty-one states, as well as the District of Columbia, Guam, Micronesia, and Puerto Rico, were using the LawHelp template.

Kaivo Software developed the Open Source Template (OST) specifically for use by TIG program grantees. States using this website have been able to build a website that addresses their specific needs in terms of content and navigation while incorporating features (such as an event calendar) that were developed to be modular and reusable. States choosing this option were advised of the importance of having an internal web service infrastructure sufficient to host the site (or a hosting agreement with an external Internet service provider) and sufficient expertise (or the capability to acquire such expertise) to maintain and enhance the site at low cost.

The development of this network of statewide legal information websites was an important step forward in the access to justice movement. As one observer commented,

> While this technology project sounds a bit prosaic, even boring, the creation of a single authentic LSC backed legal aid Web site for each and every state had profound implications. By funding statewide Web sites, [the] TIG program ensured that in each state, there was one location on the Internet where the public could find authentic legal information and ultimately legal services. . . . The program officers of LSC kept the costs of these statewide sites down, and established a floor of quality and service by insisting that most states use one of two templates for the statewide Web site. . . . These statewide sites are now a fixture of the national legal aid infrastructure. (Staudt, 2009, p. 109–110)

It soon became evident, though, that the long-term sustainability of the websites was dependent on the acquisition of additional sources of funding, as the TIG program increasingly began to focus on a range of other initiatives. In 2014, for example, Pine Tree Legal Assistance in Maine was awarded $138,000 to develop web-based expert systems to assist with resolving legal issues related to debt collection defense, and the Central Virginia Legal Aid Society was awarded $494,000 to develop a cloud-based software application to help legal aid and pro bono attorneys with case management (LSC, 2014). Other recent TIG projects focus on streamlining an increasingly diverse array of online services—for example, in 2014, the Legal Services of Greater Miami was awarded $105,000 to create a multilingual (English, Spanish, and Creole) online intake system that is to be integrated into Florida's statewide legal information website.

There are, of course, ongoing costs associated with statewide legal information websites, including software fees as well as staff to develop website content, build support for stakeholder relationships, and engage in marketing activities (Melton et al., 2005). And, as states could no longer depend on TIG funding, they made different decisions regarding how to keep their websites up and running. Accordingly, in the years since LSC first provided funding through the TIG program, the network of statewide legal information websites has evolved dramatically, with states adopting diverse approaches to both development and implementation, leading to significant variation in terms of operation, design, and content.

As the discussion in chapters 5 and 6 will demonstrate, despite fluctuations in funding, many statewide legal information websites have become an integral part of their states' access to justice strategies. They have made the transition from primarily static collections of resources (often electronic versions of print materials) and basic links to dynamic websites that often incorporate automated legal form and document preparation systems, such as A2J Guided Interviews[2] and the Interactive Community Assistance Network ("I-CAN!").[3] A growing number of sites now offer remote assistance capabilities, such as instant messaging programs that put self-help users in contact with trained specialists (Aaron, 2012; Cabral et al., 2012; Johnson, 2009; Morris, 2013; NCSC, 2006; Rhode & Bam, 2012; Staudt, 2009; Widdison, 2013; Wolf, 2012; Zorza, 2009b). Clearly, technological advancements have laid the foundation for these websites to become integrated with other legal services so that users can more easily navigate the legal system. What is less clear, however, is the extent to which these advancements are contributing to the creation of websites and online services that do, in fact, meet the needs of users who face the various barriers to information access discussed earlier in this book.

OPENING UP THE "BLACK BOX"

To address this question, it was first necessary to find out more about the development, implementation, and maintenance of statewide legal information websites, as these initiatives have not been extensively studied. In fact, the last comprehensive empirical study of statewide legal information websites was conducted in 2004 by the National Association of IOLTA Programs and the New Center for Legal Advocacy (the *2004 Statewide Legal Information Website Study*). Focused on assessing the sustainability of statewide legal information websites, this LSC-funded study used surveys and interviews to collect data from individuals working directly on the websites. The project's final report (Melton et al., 2005) described the statewide legal information websites as the "spine of the 21st century delivery system" (p. 5), noting growing acceptance of the importance of these websites. For example, 57.6 percent of survey respondents indicated that they viewed statewide legal information websites as a main vehicle for furthering access to justice goals.

The study offered insight into how the websites were being used at that time. The most frequent categories of users identified by survey respondents included community/social services organizations (88.2 percent), the general public (88.2 percent), low-income people (79.4 percent), lawyers in LSC programs (67.6 percent), and court staff (55.9 percent). The most frequently cited uses of statewide legal information websites included directories of free and low-cost legal assistance (97.1 percent), general legal information (100 percent), and self-help materials (85.3 percent).

The report also highlighted various issues pertaining to the maintenance of these sites. Support networks, such as those offered through Kaivo Open Source and Pro Bono Net, were seen as vehicles for the sharing of strategies, best practices, and lessons learned, as well as for the building of content and marketing collaborations. In terms of resources, the report stressed the importance of integrating the sites into the overall budgets of the organizations that maintain them so that they are seen as core functions rather than technology-oriented "pet projects." The hiring of dedicated staff to work specifically on content development was also viewed as important. The formation of partnerships was seen as crucial to building the necessary political support to obtain funding from third parties. The survey explored the different roles played by a number of stakeholder groups, finding that

- the most common sources of funding were LSC-funded legal services providers (56 percent), IOLTA programs (44 percent), and bar foundations (41 percent), and
- the most common in-kind supporters were LSC-funded and other legal services providers (62 percent), law schools (50 percent), pro bono programs (47 percent), and state bar associations (47 percent).

Moreover, inasmuch as libraries (59 percent), courts (68 percent), and community organizations (71 percent) were all seen as beneficiaries of statewide legal information websites, the report recommended that these entities be viewed as potential collaborators.

And, finally, the report set forth a number of key recommendations for website program staff and managers, stressing the importance of

- developing a partnership-building strategy that reaches out to potential and actual stakeholders for buy-in, content, marketing, access partnerships, evaluation, and funding;

- using grant assurances/conditions to encourage contributions by other LSC programs;
- engaging statewide funders in the practical and decision-making processes of the websites so that they have greater incentive to take responsibility for the sites;
- developing access points in courts and community organizations; and
- developing an evaluation strategy that goes beyond the self-assessments required by the LSC inasmuch as "current evaluation strategies may focus too little on short-term interim milestones, and not enough on the overall comprehensibility and utility of the site." (p. 28)

Although this survey is now over ten years old and statewide legal information websites have undergone dramatic changes during the elapsed time, its themes remain relevant and laid the foundation for my study. I, for example, was keen to learn whether the recommendations regarding partnership building and evaluation practices have been implemented.

The impetus for an updated study came from the legal services community itself. The need for research focused on statewide legal information websites is greater than ever given the central role that these initiatives are expected to play in the delivery of legal services in the future. These websites, as characterized by Staudt (2009), have the potential to serve as the "foundational building blocks for transformational delivery changes" (p. 110). Staudt's assessment appears to have merit in light of the strategy developed at the LSC Summit calling for integrated statewide portals to be built upon existing statewide legal information websites, as discussed in the introduction. In order for these websites to serve as the proverbial giant upon whose shoulders a future legal services delivery system will be built, however, we need a deeper understanding of how they were developed and, more specifically, the extent to which they were designed with the needs of users in mind. The lack of empirical research in this area is particularly problematic because, as noted by Cabral et al. (2012),

> [t]o be most effective, courts and organizations deploying access to justice technologies need to be able to build on and leverage [others'] experiences and best practices to design and implement their projects as state-of-the-art and integrated solutions, rather than reinventing the wheel and making avoidable mistakes. Beginning new projects from the strongest possible knowledge base prevents organizations from going down technology paths that end up conflicting with or excluding other valuable options and avoids wasteful mid-course corrections. (p. 313)

Accordingly, I undertook a study that sought to open up the "black box" of statewide legal information websites while highlighting both the commonalities and differences among the approaches adopted by states. The overarching purpose of this study was to build upon the existing, highly fragmented knowledge base in a way that could impact both practice and policy.

The perspectives of experts in this area—individuals involved in developing, implementing, and maintaining statewide legal information websites—served as the primary lens through which to understand how statewide legal information websites facilitate the access of self-help users, including self-represented litigants, to vital legal information. For the remainder of this book, these individuals will be referred to as "Information Providers." The study therefore was guided by the following general research questions:

RQ1: What are the principal activities that Information Providers engage in with respect to statewide legal information websites?
RQ2: What are the different ways in which states have approached these activities?
RQ3: What program development and operational issues have Information Providers faced?

The broad nature of these questions was purposeful, as the contents of the "black boxes" underlying statewide legal information websites were largely unknown at the outset of this study. In order to gather enough data for analysis, the research involved a series of interrelated data collection efforts, consisting of a pilot case study, a survey of Information Providers, and follow-up interviews with survey respondents and other Information Providers. This structure allowed for triangulation of the data, thus enhancing the validity of the study's findings (Creswell & Miller, 2000; Miles, Huberman, & Saldaña, 2014).[4] As observed by Yin (2009), the use of multiple sources of evidence allows converging lines of inquiry to develop. Here, because of the interrelated nature of the data collection efforts, many of the key themes identified early in the pilot case study were reaffirmed through the later data collection efforts. In addition, the data are linked to theoretical constructs identified in previous studies, tying together concepts from information science and legal studies to present a set of findings that coalesce around these key themes (Ryan & Bernard, 2003; Yin, 2011).

Specifically, the data collection efforts were designed to learn more about the following:

- the legal information and services currently being provided by Information Providers to benefit self-help users,
- Information Providers' understanding of target users' information needs and the barriers they face in accessing information via statewide legal information websites,
- Information Providers' knowledge regarding actual users, and
- the practices and strategies employed by Information Providers to compile and present information that they believe is needed by their users.

PILOT CASE STUDY

Case study research calls for the exploration of a bounded system or systems (Creswell, 2007). The case under examination may be an event, a process, or a program (Stake, 1995). Each statewide legal information website is an access to justice program currently serving a specific state and therefore fits within the definition of a bounded system. Given the inductive nature of the case study approach (Hamel, Dufour, & Fortin, 1993), it was a logical starting point for my investigation into the different paths followed by those working on statewide legal information websites. A pilot case study was thus conducted to develop an in-depth understanding of one state's path so as to create a baseline understanding of the different elements that come together in the development and implementation of a statewide legal information website.

Case study research requires multiple sources of information in order to provide depth to the analysis (Creswell, 2007). According to Yin (2009), there are six sources of evidence that are commonly used in case study research: documentation, archival records, interviews, direct observations, participant-observation, and physical artifacts. Given the nature of the case here (i.e., a website), the pilot case study relied primarily on two sources of evidence: interviews and documentation. Along with Information Providers, other key informants (e.g., stakeholders from throughout the legal services community and information intermediaries who use the website) were also interviewed. The case study also involved a review of relevant documentation, including website content, written procedures and protocols, promotional materials, and minutes from stakeholder meetings.

The pilot case study was a means to explore key conceptual topics that had been previously identified in a broad subject area (i.e., technology-based access to justice initiatives) (Yin, 2011, p. 31). As observed by Yin, the use of a pilot study ensures that exploratory research follows some "exploratory theory" (which he defines as the "design of research steps according to some relationship to the literature, policy issues, or other substantive source") (p. 28). Yet, at the same time, researchers using the case study method are cautioned to refrain from approaching the research problem with a firmly established theoretical perspective: "[I]nvestigators should formulate a research problem and possibly specify some potentially important variables. . . . However, they should avoid thinking about specific relationships between variables and theories as much as possible, especially at the outset of the process" (Eisenhardt, 1989, p. 536). Similar to Eisenhardt and Bourgeois's study of strategic decision making in top management teams (1988), this study began with the identification of several potentially important constructs from the relevant literature, which were used to formulate survey and interview questions. However, no assumption was made that any or all of these constructs would, in fact, be important. By refraining from making such assumptions, themes and patterns were allowed to emerge from the data, all of which were explored through subsequent data collection efforts.

The pilot case study chosen was the People's Law Library of Maryland (PLL). Key considerations included geographic proximity, PLL's longevity (Staudt, 2005), and the fact that Maryland is the first state to organize and maintain its legal information website through the state law library (Maryland Judiciary, Court Information Office, 2008). As the literature review revealed that different types of libraries are becoming increasingly active in the access to justice arena, a program in which a library was at the epicenter of a program for self-represented litigants and other self-help users was of particular interest. Notwithstanding the fact that Maryland adopted a novel approach in maintaining its statewide legal information website, an assumption was made that the issues that PLL's Information Providers have faced at different stages of development and maintenance are similar to those faced by Information Providers across the country. This assumption was based largely on the fact that the literature places PLL firmly within the existing network of statewide legal information websites: "As a result of leadership from the [LSC], every state has a statewide legal information gateway. In most states, these are administered and maintained by a coalition of organizations, and aim to comprehensiveness of content with respect to civil access to justice. Indeed, in Maryland, the statewide website . . . is operated by the State Law Library" (Zorza, 2012b, 33).

Moreover, a preliminary review of the content on PLL and other statewide legal information websites revealed similarities in terms of basic content and scope. Like many other statewide legal information websites, PLL is organized around topic areas, namely, consumer issues (e.g., contracts, debts), domestic violence, education, employment, family law, government benefits and services, health, housing, motor vehicles, senior citizens, wills/estates/probate, youth law, and other legal issues (e.g., immigration, personal injury). Within each topic area, issues of substantive law and procedure are both addressed. In addition to links to official judiciary forms, key information resources include the following:

- links to applicable laws and relevant information available through other state, as well as federal, agencies;
- research guides in a number of areas that explain how to access relevant electronic and print resources (e.g., statutes, case law, court rules, regulations, treatises, and policy documents);
- guidance regarding court processes and procedures;
- interactive quizzes to aid individuals in the decision-making process;
- a legal services directory that provides a listing of free and low-cost legal services providers; and
- a list of other resources of possible interest to self-represented litigants, including information on how to find representation, as well as links to self-help services, mediation services, and non-legal assistance/community services.

The primary goal of the pilot case study was to identify key issues and themes to explore through subsequent data collection efforts that would expand the scope of the study from Maryland to the nationwide network of statewide legal information websites. Ultimately, three main issues/themes were identified: (1) the different ways that stakeholder organizations contribute to PLL, (2) the perceived information needs of target users and the barriers they presumably face in accessing this information, and (3) the ongoing need to develop better processes for content development and maintenance of an up-to-date website.

Online Survey

Building upon the PLL pilot case study and the 2004 Statewide Legal Information Website Study, the survey sought to explore these themes and identify the different approaches taken by Information Providers across the country. In addition, a conceptual framework developed by Detlor, Hupfer, and Ruhi (2010) in a study of municipal community portals in Ontario, Canada, was instrumental in the development of this survey. Detlor et al.'s framework provides nine internal factors that influence the adoption and use of government websites: partner cooperation, ability to change internal work processes, IT workforce, funding, citizen participation in design, portal strategies and policies, leadership, marketing, and governance. During the development of survey questions, this framework proved useful to the extent that the municipal community portals, like the network of statewide legal information websites, had similar goals ("improved information access and sharing within their communities") while also exhibiting differences in terms of "technology platforms, governance structures, partner compositions and . . . IT workforce arrangements" (p. 124).

The survey contained a mixture of open- and closed-ended questions. It followed a chronological order, starting with questions about the development of the statewide legal information website before focusing on current policies and practices, such as processes for creating and updating content and the collection and analysis of user feedback. A list of survey questions can be found in appendix B. The survey was sent to a non-probability, purposive sample of Information Providers (Miles et al., 2014).[5] Using purposive sampling, the goal was to describe the range of variability that exists within the population of Information Providers (Guest, MacQueen, & Namey, 2012; Seidman, 2006). More specifically, expert sampling was the purposive sampling technique chosen because only those who have been directly involved with statewide legal information websites can offer the insights necessary to address the articulated research questions (Daniel, 2011). Seeking to reach at least one individual affiliated with each statewide legal information website, participants were recruited through contact information available on the websites, requests made through online submission forms, and the listservs maintained by Pro Bono Net and the OST communities.

Of the surveys initiated, twenty-six of them provided sufficient information to include within the sample. Of those twenty-six surveys, twenty-four were filled out by current Information Providers, and two were filled out by former Information

Providers. This sample was geographically diverse, with survey responses coming from each of the following states: Alabama, Alaska, Arkansas, California, D.C., Florida, Georgia, Idaho, Illinois, Indiana, Iowa, Maine, Massachusetts, Michigan, Minnesota, Montana, Ohio, Texas, Vermont, Washington, and West Virginia. Ten of the states from which responses were received are on the LawHelp platform maintained by Pro Bono Net.

Interviews

Interviews were held with survey respondents who indicated a willingness to participate as well as individuals recruited for the survey who expressed a preference for participating in an interview (rather than the survey). Several additional potential participants were identified during the course of the interviews. Snowball sampling (Babbie, 2013) was deemed appropriate at this stage of the data collection, as the collaboration underlying statewide legal information websites is not always readily apparent, and thus it was difficult to ascertain who (beyond the contact person designated on the website) could be a potential interview subject.

Notwithstanding the exploratory nature of this study, the ability to demonstrate consistency and stability in terms of research methods was an important consideration (Miles et al., 2014). Here, the semi-structured interviews involved a significant amount of inductive probing (Guest et al., 2012; Ryan & Bernard, 2003). An interview guide was used to ensure that a core set of topics was addressed in each interview; however, as expected, the draft interview guide evolved in "real time" during the course of each interview (Guest et al., 2012). The semi-structured interviews explored key themes from the survey in greater detail, including the roles of various stakeholders and the kinds of evaluation activities undertaken. In addition, every website was reviewed in advance to determine if any particular services or features raised questions to explore during the interviews (e.g., one site's inclusion of resources specifically for librarians).

Throughout June and July 2014, interviews were conducted with twenty-seven individuals—twenty-two interviewees were current Information Providers, one was a former Information Provider, three were staff members at Pro Bono Net, and one was a former Information Provider and former Pro Bono Net staff member. All but two of the interviews were conducted via telephone. Current Information Providers hold various professional positions, as set forth in table 4.1.

Interviewees came from the following states: Colorado, Connecticut, Florida, Idaho, Illinois, Indiana, Kansas, Massachusetts, Maine, Maryland,[6] Michigan, Montana, New Mexico, Tennessee, Texas, Vermont, and West Virginia. The purpose of the interviews with Pro Bono Net staff members was twofold: (1) to learn more about online forms (one of the features brought up frequently in the surveys),[7] and (2) to explore the role that Pro Bono Net has played—and continues to play—in fostering collaboration among statewide legal information websites.

Table 4.1. Roles of Information Providers

Roles	*Numbers of Interviewees Holding This Role*
Technology manager	3
Website manager/coordinator	5
Program/project director	4
IT staff	2
Director of organization that maintains site	4
Attorney at legal aid organization that maintains site	2
Attorney at legal organization that is affiliated with site	2

The overarching purpose of the interviews was to explore states' different paths in greater depth, honing in on key themes related to collaboration, content development and website design focused on lowering barriers to information access faced by target users, and the current state of knowledge about actual users. The interviews thus were carefully designed to examine issues related to infrastructure elements and current practices, seeking to develop a clearer idea as to how these different pieces can fit together to form a program designed to provide legal information and services to self-help users.

Twelve of the interviewees had completed the survey prior to the interview. Although the interviews with "new" interviewees included more background discussion (e.g., about the initial development of the site), the same general topics were covered in all of the interviews: the role of the LSC, funding, staffing, processes for content development and review, interactions with other organizations, outreach efforts, program evaluation, and recommendations for the future. Interviews with Information Providers who had completed the survey also involved the exploration of certain topics that emerged in response to open-ended questions. For example, several survey respondents indicated that they had worked in some capacity with libraries and/or domestic violence advocacy organizations. Accordingly, during the interviews, interviewees were asked to provide more details about these particular collaborations.

Study Limitations

This study provides insight into the different paths that states have taken in developing, implementing, and maintaining statewide legal information websites. This insight was derived primarily from data gathered from Information Providers (as well as other key informants) through the survey and interviews. In choosing this particular lens through which to study statewide legal information websites, the perspectives of users admittedly are not captured. For *this* study, however, the user perspective is not essential. Its central aim was to examine what states are doing (i.e., open up the programmatic "black box") and how they approach the different activities underlying the website. Information Providers, not users, are in the best position to answer these questions. Their perspectives on users, however, interjected user issues into this study, highlighting the need for future studies that shift the focus from Information Providers to users. Moreover, as discussed in chapter 7, a key challenge currently facing many Information Providers is their lack of connection with users. Until such time as this particular challenge is overcome, user-centered studies focused on outcomes and effectiveness will have to wait.

Arguably, another limitation of the study related to its reliance on Information Providers was the small size of this community. Out of this small community, only twenty-six surveys provided sufficient data to be included within the analysis of results. Although a concerted effort was made to design a concise survey that would pose a minimal burden on respondents, anecdotal feedback from survey respondents indicated that the length of the survey may have been a deterrent to some Information Providers. Moreover, the lower than expected response rate may have been due, at least in part, to a reluctance among legal services providers to participate in studies because of their belief that researchers do not understand the nature of their work (Charn & Selbin, 2013; Selbin et al., 2012).

When survey data is combined with interview data, however, the experiences of Information Providers from twenty-eight states—to varying degrees—were collected. Of the forty-one individuals who participated in the latter two stages of data collection, fourteen participated by survey, fifteen by interview, and twelve by both survey and interview. The combined sample reflects diversity in terms of geography, population size, and demographics (see appendix C), as well as in terms of key dimensions across which websites vary (e.g., platform, stakeholders involved). This diversity serves as a counterbalance to the relatively small sample size, allowing an understanding of the breadth of different approaches adopted by Information Providers to emerge.

And, finally, the weaknesses often associated with the use of interviews as a data collection method must be acknowledged. These weaknesses include the interviewer effect ("the sex, the age, and the ethnic origins of the interviewer have a bearing on the amount of information people are willing to divulge and their honesty about what they reveal" [Denscombe, 2007, p. 184]) and the presence of demand characteristics (when responses are influenced by the interviewee's perceptions about what is required of him or her [Gomm, 2004; Newton, 2010]). At least in the case of interviewees who also participated in the survey, however, internal consistency was evaluated by examining survey and interview data together (Newton, 2010).

It is important to remember that research efforts in the area of technology-enabled access to justice initiatives remain at a nascent stage. Because the amount of research that has been conducted to date on statewide legal information websites in particular is extremely limited, there are more questions than answers at this time. No one study can provide answers to all of those questions, but that fact did not deter me from opening a line of inquiry with potentially far-reaching consequences for legal services providers and self-help users.

The goal of the study was to paint a detailed picture of the complexities surrounding the development, implementation, and operation of statewide legal information websites. Looking across the themes that emerged from the data collected during the three stages of this study, the value of this study clearly lies in its implications for policy and practice. The immediate outcome thus is a set of recommendations to guide future policy making and practice with respect to statewide legal information websites. These recommendations, which will be presented in chapter 7, are intended to serve as a much-needed bridge between research and practice. Statewide legal information websites, like all access to justice initiatives, exist to close the justice gap that currently prevents far too many people living in this country from receiving the legal assistance they need. Now, more than ever, recommendations supported by empirical research are crucial as statewide legal information websites are increasingly viewed as the foundation for the next wave of technology-based access to justice initiatives.

Without an understanding of what does and does not matter in the development and implementation of statewide legal information websites, there is likely to be unnecessary trial and error. As noted by Cabral et al. (2012), "[d]eveloping concrete mechanisms for better collection, curation, and dissemination of knowledge, experience, guidance, case studies, and best practices would be a valuable step toward lowering the knowledge barrier and promoting technology implementation that is holistic and strategic" (p. 315). This study, by developing recommendations built upon the knowledge acquired by those who have played a crucial role in building the existing network of statewide legal information websites, was intended to serve as an important step in lowering this barrier. While Information Providers are the immediate beneficiaries of this enhanced knowledge sharing, those who are currently denied equal access to justice ultimately stand to reap the greatest benefits from technology-enabled self-help services that are optimally designed, implemented, and operated to meet their needs.

NOTES

1. A complete list of current LSC grantees can be found at http://www.lsc.gov/grants-grantee-resources/our-grantees.

2. Developed in 2005 by the Center for Access to Justice and Technology at Chicago-Kent College of Law and the Center for Computer-Assisted Legal Instruction (CALI), A2J Guided Interviews employs HotDocs document assembly software to build a form based on the user's answers, utilizing one of the approximate 2,300 templates stored on the national LawHelp Interactive (LHI) server (Cabral et al., 2012).

3. Since the program was developed by the Legal Aid Society of Orange County, seven states have adopted it and almost two hundred thousand pleadings have been uploaded. This

system is explicitly designed for individuals with limited computer experience and literacy skills (e.g., employing audio prompts for each question).

4. Among qualitative researchers, there is debate about the use of the term "validity" (see, e.g., Patton, 2002; Stenbacka, 2001). The need to demonstrate the "truth value" of a qualitative study, however, is not contested: "Do the findings of the study make sense? Are they credible to the people we study and to our readers? Do we have an authentic portrait of what we were looking at?" (Miles et al., 2014).

5. The online survey was launched during the first week of March 2014 and remained in the field for seven weeks.

6. Individuals currently working on the People's Law Library of Maryland were interviewed at this time so as to explore the themes identified through the survey.

7. Pro Bono Net, in collaboration with LSC and the Ohio State Legal Services Association, maintains LHI, a website developed to facilitate document assembly initiatives across the country.

5

Opening Up the "Black Box" of Statewide Legal Information Websites

The pilot case study discussed in chapter 4 opened up the programmatic "black box" of one statewide legal information website. Drawing upon themes identified through this initial effort, the subsequent survey and interviews led to the development of a more nuanced understanding of the existing network of statewide legal information websites through a study of the people involved in different aspects of the development, implementation, and maintenance of these sites. This understanding was refined through the survey and then the interviews as various questions related to "how?" came to the surface:

- How do Information Providers address issues related to content development, website design, outreach, and evaluation?
- How do Information Providers seek to overcome the barriers to information access they have identified?
- How do Information Providers work with various access to justice stakeholders?
- How do statewide legal information websites fit within the broader access to justice realm of which they are a part?

And so the principal activities of Information Providers were identified, and differences were observed in terms of how Information Providers engage in each of these activities. These differences stem from the fact that no two Information Providers have the same level of resources, nor the same amount of support from the legal services community, nor the same relationships with the various organizations that comprise the access to justice community. Notwithstanding these differences, one common thread among Information Providers emerged: they are committed to continually improving their websites so that users are able to access a range of information that can help them address the legal problem(s) that brought them to the website in the first place. Many Information Providers, however, have limited information about their users' experiences with the website. This lack of connection between Information Providers and website users impedes evaluation efforts, raising questions about the ability of the access to justice community to assess the impact of statewide legal information websites.

As the study unfolded, there was a shift from thinking about statewide legal information websites as technology projects that exist within the access to justice realm to conceiving of them as access to justice initiatives that employ technology to deliver information and services to a defined group of users. People—through their collaborative efforts in content development and outreach, as well as their perspectives on user needs based on their personal experiences working with self-represented litigants—are the driving force behind these websites. Moreover, the challenges they have faced, and continue to face, cannot be solved by technology alone but rather through ongoing collaborative efforts to facilitate access to legal information and services through technology-enabled means.

These challenges are central to this chapter's discussion of study findings related to (1) the environment in which statewide legal information websites exist, and (2) the different activities in which Information Providers engage to sustain and improve the websites. In chapter 6, we will turn our attention to the role of collaboration in overcoming challenges in facilitating access to online legal information by those who most need it.

THE SURROUNDING ENVIRONMENT

Each statewide legal information website is a product of its environment, which is comprised of internal elements (i.e., the infrastructure built up around it) and external elements (i.e., the legal services community that surrounds it, as well as the broader economic and political forces that impact this community). The infrastructure surrounding statewide legal information websites is comprised of two main elements—funding and staffing. Study participants confirmed that the LSC, through the TIG program, was initially a primary source of funding in many states. For those states without an existing website, the sizeable grants offered by LSC in the early years (approximately $500,000, according to one Information Provider) created the impetus to develop an online presence. Other states used early TIG money to bolster their existing online presence through outreach, partnership building, and related activities or to build up an infrastructure around the website (e.g., create an IT support position). Since that time, states have continued to use TIG money to expand outreach efforts as well as to undertake technology projects.

Study participants, however, made it clear that TIG money did not remain the sole—or even a primary—source of funding for long, forcing them to find alternative means to support the continued operation of their websites. Several different approaches to dealing with this transition were identified throughout the interviews.

The approach adopted by legal services organizations in several states has been to treat the website essentially as an operating cost and move it "in house." In some cases, Information Providers now use grant funds received for broader initiatives to make related website enhancements:

> Right now, [money] comes from wherever we can get it from . . . you can see a DV [domestic violence] helpline on our site, we use the funding from that grant to upgrade the information on that service that we provide. If there's foreclosure information, we use that funding and so on and so forth. But, there's no funding dedicated to this website right now.

Among those who continue to seek external support for the operation of the website, state bar foundations were most frequently cited as an important source of funding. Other sources of funding mentioned by study participants include the SJI, a non-profit corporation established by federal law[1]; general LSC funds; state government agencies; lawyers' trust funds (i.e., IOLTA); and donations from law firms and individuals. State government money, in some instances, has been tied to certain initiatives, such as health care and mortgage foreclosure settlement. One of the most recent statewide legal information websites to launch was originally funded with TIG money but is now funded by a local chapter of a national non-profit trade association. At the time of the interviews, that organization had approximately $17,000 in funding to maintain a statewide website for social services referral information. Through this partnership, the legal services organization developed a website that includes both social services and legal information and continues to use available funds to maintain and market the site.

Often, discussions of the fluidity of funding sources segued into broader discussions about the instability of the legal services environment. It was in fact this instability that spurred the initial development of statewide legal information websites in some states. The political environment of the 1980s drove some legal services providers to consider more cost-effective means of service delivery.[2]

> Well, one of the things that precipitated our moving to the Internet, were funding cuts . . . for the program as a whole. I'm not real good at time but . . . sometime during the Reagan years, there was a threat that we would be reduced to zero funding and we just didn't know what our future was going to be, what service we would be able to continue to provide and we viewed this as a way that, if we were severely cut back, we could still provide a level of service to our clients with the fewest personnel, if you will, that we would need to maintain that level of service.

More recently, the economic climate of the past few years has ushered in another wave of budgetary contractions within the legal services community. The result for some Information Providers has been unstable levels of funding, often leading to prohibitively small budgets. Fluctuating interest rates were also identified as a problem—for example, funds available from IOLTA programs have been adversely impacted by low interest rates. Not surprisingly, statewide legal information websites in those states where funds are no longer earmarked for the site have been particularly hard hit.

Due to these funding constraints, many Information Providers find themselves in a difficult position. They would like to do more but, without additional funding, improvements and additions are not feasible. They can articulate what they would like to incorporate into the site (e.g., interactive features, such as online chat) and previous outreach efforts they would like to revive (e.g., to domestic violence shelters and senior centers), but they recognize that all of these efforts require more money than is currently available. As described by one Information Provider discussing the challenge of locating sufficient resources to develop multimedia content: "[M]y budget is tiny and so, you know, if I'm working on a video, it can be challenging to find a place to shoot. If I want to find art, it's expensive to get stock art so trying to create something out of nothing can be a bit challenging."

In many cases, external grant funding is the only option for those Information Providers who are looking to turn their aspirations into reality. Many of these projects involve Information Providers working with access to justice stakeholders within their state, as well as other Information Providers and organizations across the country, to do things that would likely be impossible to accomplish on their own. One study participant, for example, enthusiastically talked about two TIG applications that were currently pending—one for developing an online game with a local university, and one for working with law students to create online tutorials for self-represented litigants that could be used by legal aid organizations in other states.

Current funding constraints tie directly into the staffing issues that many study participants discussed. The general sentiment among most Information Providers is that they currently are the only ones in the organization whose *primary* responsibility is the website. Generally speaking, however, others contribute content and/or work on technical issues related to the site. Administrative support personnel or "tech folks" within the organization, for example, often provide assistance with posting content to the site and related tasks. Other interviewees described a situation in which everything related to the website flows through them, with one describing herself as the "conductor" of the site. These individuals effectively function as gatekeepers: "What you really need to do is, as the one putting stuff up, is sort of wade through all of it and say 'well, this would be really good,' 'that can just stay on their website' . . . and then what you do is try to fill the gaps in." A couple of websites, however, are fortunate enough to have a number of dedicated staff—Information Providers working on two statewide legal information websites described having dedicated staffs of twelve and five individuals, respectively. The former, for example, has a dedicated legal content manager for both the English and Spanish versions of the website.

Study participants were asked if they felt they had adequate staffing and funding—the term "adequate" was generally interpreted to mean enough to keep the site up and running. While many Information Providers initially indicated that they felt that the site, in its current form, was sustainable, they then clarified their response to stress that limited staffing and funding were impeding efforts to enhance their sites in any number of ways, including through the development of additional content or outreach efforts. As one study participant mused, "Do we have enough people so that we have a functioning website, which we are more or less able to keep current? Yes. . . . Could we have a much more robust site, could we have a lot more content on the public access [site], in particular, if we have more people dealing with it? Oh, yes." One Information Provider offered the following assessment of these challenges:

> [H]ere's the thing about the website . . . that I think sometimes people lose sight of . . . people look at technology and they think it's this magic bullet, [but] it's only as good as the people you've got working on it. So, we have enough staff to keep it going but we're getting more staff to really do more. . . . [I]t requires man hours as far as tedious work—let's update this resource . . . making sure the links still work and making sure that everything is there. I mean, at a certain point, a website is just a delivery system.

The law is not static and so these sites cannot be static. Having outdated forms on the website, by way of example, can have adverse impacts for self-help users if the clerk's office refuses to accept a filing because an improper form is used. One Pro Bono Net staff member observed that sustainability in this context involves maintaining an updated website, the costs of which (in terms of both time and money) are not always adequately considered at the outset: "But, the other thing too is to realize is that these things cost money . . . don't start a project that you're not going to sustain. Don't put a form out there that you're not going to have the wherewithal to change when the law changes."

It was comparatively easy to think strategically about the website when states were able to fund a dedicated staff person through the TIG program. While a few states continue to have one or more individuals whose sole responsibility is working on the site, this does not appear to be the norm. Although there is significant variation in this area, there is still typically a "point person" for the site, but that person is finding himself or herself spread very thin these days, as the legal services community finds itself in a state of continual contraction. That person is often responsible for other projects that may or may not be related to the website:

> [I]t might be "OK, now you're coordinating the LiveHelp project" or "Now, you're also going to be managing the development of multimedia videos or of online forums." . . . [B]ecause . . . dedicated funding is no longer available from LSC and the funding contractions in the field in general, I think that those coordinator positions are now wearing many more hats than they were in their early days.

In one sense, giving the Information Provider responsibility for a suite of related initiatives fits well with the idea of integrating the website into the core activities of the organization. For some, the idea of integration is not new—several Information Providers indicated that, from the beginning, the website was conceived as a way to share information with those potential clients to whom they could not provide direct services and, ideally, enable them to deal with their legal problems on their own. This mind-set encourages Information Providers, as well as others within the organization, to view the website as another means of service delivery to the client population, potentially paving the way for it to be an important component of an online triage system. The addition of other responsibilities to the Information Provider's workload, however, forces them to make decisions about where to devote their time and energy. Conceivably, the website can fall to the wayside as other, more immediate needs demand staff members' attention. One Information Provider described how his efforts to go forward with automated documents—something he believes will significantly improve the website—languished for several years because there was no one person devoted to this particular project.

Moreover, as noted earlier, some organizations now treat the site as part of their general operating costs, whereas others depend on external grant money to create new content, add new features, and otherwise keep the site up to date and relevant. Both of these scenarios raise issues related to sustainability. For Information Providers in the former group, it can be difficult to maintain the visibility of the site and make a convincing case that additional resources should be devoted to it. It depends, in large part, on the extent to which decision makers (both within and outside of the organizations) see the value of the website as compared to the value of traditional services:

> [I]t is the priority for [the legal services organization] . . . we're going to fight tooth and nail to keep the website. I know that we've made . . . personnel decisions and human resources decisions based on, you know, do we lose the website or do we lose, you know, a staff position? Our board is very protective of the website because it does serve so many people.

A reliance on external grant money also raises questions about the long-term outlook for the website. As noted by one former Information Provider,

> I think that that is the challenge for most programs, particularly the part afterwards of being able to maintain the content. And . . . I don't have a really good solution for that—it's just an area that particularly after the grant runs out, I have a feeling that there's a lot of content out there that doesn't get updated . . . either because they've contracted out and haven't planned for future updates or just because priorities change and . . . staff turn over and some of the content is forgotten.

These staffing issues tie directly into another challenge observed by numerous Information Providers—the lack of buy-in from others within the organization. Several study participants recounted their early struggles to convince their co-workers to embrace the use of technology in the delivery of legal services. As described by one Information Provider, "we had to learn how to use and maximize the capabilities of the site—so it was on us to take the tools and try them and use them in new ways to support our work. So, the challenge was internal (adapting to new tools and change) rather than a challenge with the tools. It was a cultural shift that we had to go through." Particularly in the early years, Information Providers also had to address lawyers' questions about the extent to which providing information on the Internet was tantamount to providing legal advice.

Years later, Information Providers report that this problem persists as they meet with resistance from people within their organizations who remain skeptical of technology or who have a limited understanding of it. As described by one study participant, "generally as a body, [and] there are plenty of exceptions to this, but as a body, the legal services grantee organizations have not grasped the concept that the legal profession is moving to an electronic-based, online-based delivery. So, there's resistance in the leadership, probably because they don't really get it. I'm not saying that they're not forward-thinking; I'm thinking that they just don't get it." Along the same line, other Information Providers described lingering apprehension among staff members about developing a social media presence.

PRINCIPAL ACTIVITIES

Related to these differences in terms of both funding and staffing are differences in terms of how Information Providers approach four main activities related to the website, as identified through the survey and then the interviews: content development and review, website design, outreach, and evaluation. Before discussing these various activities, it is worth noting that almost every aspect of Information Providers' work focuses on, to one extent or another, user needs. There is variation in terms of how the study participants defined their users, however. The survey, for example, asked respondents to specify who originally used the site. Among the most frequently provided responses were "low-income individuals," "the general public," "self-represented litigants," and "legal services providers and information intermediaries." References to target users (past and present), however, tended to focus on one or more subsets of this broad audience: low-income individuals, individuals with "low literacy," "self-represented [or pro se] litigants," and/or LEP individuals. Some Information Providers take an even narrower view of their target audience, focusing on clients (presumably, clients of the legal aid organization that maintains the website).

CONTENT DEVELOPMENT AND REVIEW

In speaking about the various activities involved in currently maintaining a statewide legal information website, Information Providers focused primarily on what they are doing to create new content and update existing content. Early on, there was a tendency to treat statewide legal information websites as "clearinghouses," storing any and all legal information for self-help users. Some states have moved further away from this model than others. While there is now a growing emphasis on quality over quantity, there is still a fair amount of cleanup work to be done on many sites. As described by one former Information Provider,

> most people went for breadth over sort of some really good content and so we had, I think that there were ten different areas that we were looking at in terms of content and that certainly—family law was a priority. . . . [B]ut there were still other [areas] like . . . social security related things, disability law, [and] education. Those sorts of things that were included on there but generally were fairly poorly covered. And I wonder sort of, in thinking back, if . . . instead of spending the resources on trying to review those extra pieces of content that were very sort of light, not focused . . . and didn't necessarily always answer the questions that people were coming to our site for, we had focused more . . . on divorce and parenting plans, on . . . adoption things . . . on landlord tenant issues, and those consumer law issues—that they might not have improved more quickly.

A Pro Bono Net staff member agreed with this assessment, observing that the early impulse to aggregate all possible legal information left many websites with "dead weight." She noted, however, that the clearinghouse approach made more sense early on because other organizations in the non-profit sector were not maintaining that information, and so the legal services organizations were meeting an important community need.

A key element of transitioning away from the clearinghouse model involves focusing on helping users solve their specific problems rather than providing information of a more general nature. This shift, however, makes the site a more labor-intensive venture, as it is easier to provide links to other websites than to craft detailed guidance that walks users through the steps they must take in order to address a specific legal situation. Their efforts to provide users with this type of assistance have made Information Providers increasingly aware of the myriad barriers that their users may face in their efforts to access information. Limited literacy, limited English-language proficiency, and lack of understanding of legal terminology were the most frequently cited barriers in survey responses. Other noted barriers included lack of Internet access, lack of digital literacy, and disabilities (e.g., visual/hearing impairments).

The lack of understanding of legal terminology, in particular, is an integral part of one of the biggest challenges facing Information Providers—how do you help non-lawyers locate information that can help them address their legal problems? In addition to trying to grasp basic legal concepts, they may be struggling to locate information that addresses separate but related legal issues, or they may not even understand that their problem is in fact legal in nature. Thus, it is not surprising that the importance of "plain language" was stressed in survey responses (see table 5.1) as well as throughout the interviews. Overall, study participants demonstrated an acute awareness of the importance of providing content that is written at a level appropriate for target users and of explaining legal terminology and concepts in a way that is understandable to laypersons.

Table 5.1. **Plain-Language Issues (Sample Responses)**

Survey Question	*Sample Responses*
Please describe any unexpected obstacles that were encountered during the initial development of the site.	"Recognizing the challenge of putting legal information in comprehensible (i.e., reading level of sixth–eighth grade) format."
What measures have you taken to address these challenges [to the development of website content]?	"I will not publish most information that does not meet a certain level of plain language. There are exceptions, but for the most part . . . [w]e edit and edit and edit until we get it to the reading level we need." "Our content development staff have been trained in how to write in plain language, and we strive to keep all content at a sixth-grade reading level to keep all content accessible to self-represented people. We brainstorm together to try to simplify concepts; we outline our content to keep a tight scope of focus." "The Legal Content Editor is trained in plain-language writing and has reviewed and rewritten most existing content applying these techniques."
Please briefly describe actions undertaken to overcome [barriers].	"[We] make every effort to deliver information in Plain English. We strive for an eighth-grade reading level on the Flesch-Kincaid scale." "Keeping the reading level at sixth grade to be accessible for low-literacy individuals . . . [and] defining all legal terminology used. . . . [We also] built a lexicon into the site to give descriptions of commonly used words." "[O]ur goal is 70 to 80 on the Flesch Reading Ease score, which is approximately seventh-grade level."

Numerous Information Providers, however, noted that legal professionals often struggle with this aspect of writing content. The following two quotes aptly illustrate this point:

- "We still tend to think like lawyers—analyzing every possibility and trying to prepare people for every possibility—which may end up confusing people in the end."
- "So many of them just throw something together with no or little commitment or understanding that 80 percent of English-speaking American adults cannot read proficiently above the seventh-grade level. There is very little commitment on the part of many editors to ensuring that the material they dash off in a hurry is actually useful to many of our readers."

Study participants—having identified key barriers to information access—were also eager to share their ideas for improving their sites to better meet users' information needs. Study participants focused on two ideas in particular: incorporating new technologies (e.g., document assembly, online intake, guided interviews, triage) to present content in different formats and making the sites more useful for LEP individuals. This is highlighted by the current projects described by Information Providers, examples of which are presented in table 5.2.

In terms of interactive features, online forms, by far, were discussed most frequently. One Pro Bono Net staff member emphasized the central role of interactive forms in the access to justice movement, characterizing them as an "essential underpinning" to courts' efforts to become more open to the public. The growth in this area has been significant—for example, Pro Bono Net now supports forty-five states with approximately four thousand LawHelp Interactive (LHI) online forms and interviews. A study participant offered the following description of recent work in this area:

> I've been working mostly with the document assembly—various kinds of document assembly. [We do] two kinds of documents—one based on . . . interactive PDF documents and the other based on HotDocs programming. [The PDFs are] . . . JavaScript programmed behind the scenes to do complex calculations . . . [the state] child support guidelines are really complex and very difficult particularly for somebody who's poorly educated who is trying to handle their own case in court. . . . The PDF documents . . . became really the standard for, at least for the family law ones, the standard for the entire bar—not only our client population used them but lots of the . . . family law bar in the state began using them.

Funding, however, remains an issue here as well, as described by one Information Provider who received funding to produce templates for frequently used family law documents. Through this experience, they learned "that document assembly requires a significant commitment of resources, to have a staff person with substantial (if not

Table 5.2. Projects Currently in Development

Type of Project	Description
Online intake system	"[W]e have . . . a current TIG [to build] a portal through our public website, where people can apply online for . . . services through the LSC-funded programs in [the state]."
Online triage system	"We're working with [Pro Bono Net and others] . . . to build a server that will direct clients . . . to simple interviews we can come up with for at least the four major areas that most clients come to us for and that's family law, housing law, consumer law, and . . . public benefits cases and then try . . . to match up their responses in ways that also looks at the geographic data and the demographic data to try to make the best guess at which agency is going to actually provide the service to them so we get it right the first time and not bounce them around from one place to another."
Interactive tools	"I'm working with [a] game design department . . . to build a game—a serious game—it's in quotes, a "serious game"—for . . . self-represented parties going to court—what to expect to do, what to do, how to address the judge, how to submit evidence."
Portals	"[W]e're going to have four indexed mini-portals—one in English, one in Chinese, one in Vietnamese, and one in Spanish. . . . [S]o what we're going to do is put [translated content that] cover[s] most of what you would need if you're coming to [the website] and . . . you click one button and you'll see a variety of information available on a variety of issues in your language."
Online classrooms	"[W]hat we would be doing is partnering with [CALI] to take our online classrooms, which are sort of a next generation of online learning [and] . . . build a national site which CALI will over time maintain—where legal aid programs and . . . law schools can partner up—it would serve as sort of a repository for classrooms."

full-time) assignment to developing and maintaining document assembly templates and interviews."

Other interactive features mentioned include online intake and chat services. Online intake is viewed as increasingly necessary, as evidenced by the number of states who have already implemented it or are planning to do so in the foreseeable future. As observed by one Information Provider, "I think that more and more people are accessing services online and so I think it's important for the legal aid organizations to offer that as an option that also has the advantage of being open all the time, right? I think there's an impression that legal aid offices are closed all the time or that they're not available or that the hotlines . . . you know, you call and you're on hold for 30 minutes or whatever . . . online technology is so scalable and that meets a need." This idea of wanting to provide "around the clock" legal assistance has also arisen within the context of online chat services (e.g., LiveHelp). Clearly, these services would require additional staffing, and questions persist about the feasibility of enhancing services in this manner. As suggested by one Information Provider, one possible solution is to build a volunteer program that would not only expand weekday hours for LiveHelp but also make the service available on the weekend.

In terms of language accessibility, the strides that Information Providers are able to make in terms of multilingual content are largely dependent upon available resources. Little uniformity thus can be seen in the approaches taken by states. Three states have recently added Spanish-language mirror sites. A fourth state has developed mirror sites in six of the most frequently spoken non-English languages and, in connection therewith, the Information Provider is currently devoting staff resources to the management and oversight of translation-related activities (e.g., having an AmeriCorps member maintain a spreadsheet to track activities and expenditures related to translations). The more limited approaches taken by other states fall into two categories: using machine translation and providing a selection of content in the most popular languages. One Information Provider who has adopted the former approach explained how they made the decision to highlight certain languages into which the site can be translated:

> So we basically polled our offices—what are the main languages you see people coming in or people calling from that they speak. . . . Google allows for fifty or so different languages and we didn't want to have just a huge long list that people would have to scroll through to find their language. We may have inadvertently left a few people out—a small minority—but we decided, based on those polls of our local offices, these were the primary languages besides English that are spoken in our state and those would primarily be the people looking at our website. We know it's not the best translation—it's a machine translation, but it's better than nothing.

Manual translation requires expertise that may not reside within the organization that maintains the website. One interviewee described a collaborative approach to translating select content wherein he has been working with an undergraduate Spanish translation class. After the instructor of that class engaged in several rounds of translation work with the students, the Information Provider received the translations electronically which were then reviewed by court translators and others with similar expertise. The feedback received to date has been very positive, and the Information Provider is now considering this pilot project as a model for future translation (and other content development) work.

In addition to the effort expended to develop new content that better meets user needs, Information Providers discussed the importance of ensuring that information provided on their websites remains up to date and relevant. As states continue their transition away from the clearinghouse model, Information Providers are taking a close look at existing content to determine whether it still furthers the site's mission.

By way of example, one Information Provider discussed several ways that he planned to improve the organization of information on the site, such as highlighting the most in-demand content by creating an "essential information" section and weeding out single-page flyers/brochures that provide too little information to be of any real assistance. He explained,

> One of the problems you face with . . . statewide legal websites—is that first you start off with not enough information but then you get too much. You don't want to take any down because it's valuable, so what you have to start doing is start highlighting information that will help most people. . . . So we try to make sure that the stuff we're going to highlight is the best stuff and the stuff that's easy to understand. And we're going to show them that there is real information here, then we can link them in. Once they know there is something real here, then they are more inclined to stay and really find information that they need.

More than half of survey respondents indicated that there is a process in place for identifying needed changes and updates to the website. The open-ended survey responses revealed that there was a fair amount of variation in these processes, running the gamut from ad hoc review to highly formalized processes. Early efforts to encourage people to get involved in content development and to institutionalize stakeholder support through advisory committees met with varying degrees of success. Regardless of their success (or lack thereof), however, many of these early efforts have been replaced by increasingly informal ways of conducting business related to the website. Only a few states currently have carefully documented procedures that require action on the part of various staff members as well as outside substantive experts.

Study participants from the states with formal processes offered detailed descriptions of the quality assurance procedures implemented to ensure that content review occurs at regularly scheduled intervals. As noted by one Information Provider, "[w]e have a Quality Assurance process that flags each piece of content for review on an annual basis. Each item of content is assigned to one or more content editors, who receive e-mails that review is due. They conduct a form of review (either plain language, or substantive, or links review) and publish the changes to the website." For many of the states in which one person is responsible for the day-to-day operations of the site, however, formal processes are now viewed as superfluous. One study participant explained,

> Early on, we did create some written protocols about content review, content contribution, all that sort of thing. But, the reality was that we never—we, I should say I—was never able to get enough different people involved in contributing on a repeating basis that those protocols contributed to efficiency. They didn't. I was the one who was doing it and so I was the one who was able to look through pieces—review both for substantive accuracy and for readability, usefulness in terms of who the intended audience was going to be.

In addition, there was significant variation in terms of what Information Providers consider content review. Among the different forms it can take are the following:

- checking links to make sure they are still live ("I check all the links every couple of months");
- verifying that any changes to the law are reflected in site content ("[W]e do . . . a thorough review at the end of every [state legislative] session of all the statutes and that's mostly where our updates come from");
- tagging content with a date to keep track of when it was last updated ("Every piece of content that's added to the website is tagged with [the] person's name who created it and a review date. And so, on that date, that person gets an e-mail that says, 'Your content needs to be reviewed.' And it's basically once a year"); and,
- ensuring that calendar events are up to date ("We do have a section on legal clinics in the community that is updated every month").

Through these discussions of what is involved with content development and review, it became evident that these particular activities are very much impacted by the funding and staffing issues described in the previous section. For example, an increasing reliance on external grant money creates stress for at least some Information Providers as they find themselves needing to shape content development around grant-funded projects, which may or may not align with the needs of their target users. One interviewee, for example, opined that LSC's emphasis on mobile app development a few years ago was somewhat of a misfire:

> [W]e jumped in early on the apps . . . to just again experiment and so we did this national legal aid news app and a national legal aid finder app. The first one got into both doors, but the second one—Apple kind of turned up their noses at. It wasn't entertaining enough. And it wasn't "appy" enough. . . . I think that apps have their place and can fit for very specific targeted sorts of purposes, but I think generally having experimented with apps, that we have more recently put more effort into responsive design . . . and we've more recently again put more emphasis on that [rather] than more app development.

By and large, though, limited staff resources have created the most turmoil for Information Providers. In almost every case, the staff members (from within the organization that maintains the site) and volunteers from other organizations that assist the Information Provider with the site are overburdened. Interviewees described situations in which legal services attorneys are too busy serving their clients to develop content for the site, or they initially express interest in developing content but then fail to follow through. As described by one study participant, "[w]e struggle to get timely responses from subject matter experts (who are usually busy legal aid attorneys) to help us substantively update our content."

Respondents, however, were sympathetic to the time constraints with which legal services and other volunteer attorneys were dealing: "[Legal services] staff are the best providers of content but have little time to develop content." This quote highlights one of the key reasons identified by respondents for current problems in the content review process—they want "subject matter experts" to be involved in the process, but these individuals often struggle to balance the many demands on their time. According to several respondents, these time constraints have made it exceedingly difficult to maintain an up-to-date and accurate website:

- "With a small staff (1), it is difficult to maintain all of our content. Although some staff attorneys, attorneys from other projects, private attorneys, AAGs [assistant attorney generals], and law students all pitch in, we are always scrambling to keep everything current."
- "We engage law student interns to serve as content assistants," but "with thousands of pieces of content, this is a difficult task."
- "We tend to rely on legal aid attorneys who are committed to make sure when the law changes, the material on the website is updated or written to reflect changes and who take stuff down if it is inaccurate. Even so, it can take us two years to update content after the law changes."

Volunteers, as well as staff members, can pose challenges. Information Providers described varying levels of success in finding suitable volunteers. As explained by a former Information Provider, the problem was twofold—they lacked a clear idea of how to use volunteers and struggled to find individuals who had a genuine interest in working on the site. For those who currently work with volunteers, the issue is often one of fit—while they are grateful for any assistance that people are willing to give, several study participants also indicated that volunteers with expertise in certain areas, who can apply this expertise to the task of updating content, were highly sought after yet often elusive. One Information Provider described the predicament in the following manner:

> I don't think that that's something that makes sense to have, you know, new attorneys and things like—people who we just appeal to on a sheer goodwill, pro bono basis to do because I think that it's terribly inefficient—they don't know any more than I do about that. I mean, I'm trained as an attorney and so I can struggle my way through any given page but we have hundreds of them. . . . The magic bullet as far as I can tell in my head would be a very experienced attorney who does something all the time, who [is] attuned to changes in the law in their own practice. . . . They can read down and say either yea or nay and if nay . . . they can do a little draft up of it then. I think that, with the right person, that's more like a half hour process than a major research assignment.

Another Information Provider echoed this sentiment, explaining how student interns generally lack an understanding of both the legal and technical issues (and are not there long enough to receive the necessary training), thus limiting the projects to which she can assign them. While acknowledging that interns can help by generating new ideas and testing different features, a long-term volunteer who could provide assistance with all aspects of the site would be more valuable.

Other Information Providers described volunteer fatigue—people are continually being asked to help out more to make up for the funding and staffing reductions that so many legal services organizations are facing, and it is becoming increasingly difficult to find people who are willing to take on yet another commitment. As one interviewee explained, "Maybe I can come up with a couple of people that have a grant with an outreach component and then they'll really get fired up? But, at this point, we're asking people in grantee programs who are already volunteering for clinics, and they're already volunteering for community ed. . . . And, at some point, even I don't want to do any more volunteering."

And, finally, the ongoing struggle of finding people to do content review and revision work in a timely manner has led several respondents to deviate from (and in some cases, abandon) any processes that they may have put in place. As noted by one study participant, "[m]ost structured plans for promoting more content contribution from others have not worked well. As a result, I've pretty much resorted to only ad hoc 'grab someone when I see them doing something related' and can convince them to convert it to web-appropriate information." The frustration felt by several Information Providers was evident, with one listing a variety of strategies her organization had implemented ("paying people to develop/edit content, pairing them with law students for support, formally recognizing volunteers, and more") before concluding that "none have been totally successful, and it remains hard." The absence of formal processes can be a cause for concern to the extent that it allows work associated with the site to become less defined (e.g., content is developed on a "catch as catch can" basis), which can lead to a neglected site. A neglected site, in turn, may lead others within the organization, as well as external funders, to question its value.

Website Design

Many of the study participants did not directly work on website design, as it is often handled by either an IT support person within the organization who maintains the site or an outside contractor. As a result, this topic was discussed in rather general terms, such as when Information Providers were providing background information on the development of the site.

These discussions, however, were enlightening as they highlighted study participants' understanding of the continually evolving nature of statewide legal information websites. For example, the majority of survey respondents indicated that their statewide legal information websites have undergone at least one significant revision, defined as "changes to the overall design of the site as well as site content." In some cases, these revisions have been very extensive, impacting everything from the content management system to navigation to search functionality to language accessibility. Notwithstanding these revisions, study participants provided a number of reasons as to why they still do not consider their current websites to be particularly user-friendly, including the organization of information, navigation issues, poor search functionality, or some combination of the three. As noted by one Information Provider, "[o]ne of the major changes with the relaunch is to make the site more user-friendly and better organized so that resources do not appear in categories for which they are peripherally, at best, relevant." Several study participants noted that the root of the problem was the overall quantity of information, which made navigation of the site cumbersome. Thus, they are focused on streamlining content so as to provide only that information which is perceived to be the most helpful:

- "With the launch of the new LH3 platform, we have removed sections covering topics for which we do not represent clients and therefore cannot adequately maintain. . . . We also removed non-legal community resource materials, again, as we cannot keep this current, and there now exist other resources, such as 211, to fill this need."
- "We are working on implementing a 'quality over quantity' strategy which would cut down on the amount of resources, but make sure that no useful information is lost. So instead of five one-page pamphlets, there would be one comprehensive guide covering the same area of law. More comprehensive information and less flyers."

Information Providers also commented on how the fast-moving nature of technology requires them to constantly think about the next redesign of the site in an effort to keep up with the latest trends. One respondent indicated that she was happy with the current design of the site but acknowledged that "it is a fast-moving world and, to keep up, we'll have to redesign in a few years, if not sooner."

Across the board, the foremost technological advancement on which study participants are currently focused is mobile technology and the related issue of responsive design. Only half of the survey respondents indicated that their site is currently compatible with mobile devices. Of those who work on a site that is not currently mobile compatible, several Information Providers recognized that this was a barrier that needed to be addressed, citing an increasing use of mobile devices by low-income and rural users as the impetus for their current efforts to design a mobile-responsive site.

Evaluation

Statewide legal information websites generally collect usage data. This data is generally reviewed on a regular basis, with the majority of study participants indicating that review occurs at least once a month or once every six months. Among those Information Providers who discussed what they learned through examining usage statistics, almost all of them specifically referenced Google Analytics. In addition to

Google Analytics, data can be obtained specifically about the use of online forms (e.g., how many people started filling out a form, how many people completed the process) as well as through an online intake system. As to the latter, one Information Provider has been working with her IT support staff to collect this data because she was "interested in the breakdown of cases, both cases we accept but more importantly cases we don't take or just provide advice to . . . in terms of topics, age and location so that we can better respond to those issues on our website."

In general, site usage data yields insights into several key trends, including the following:

1. Site growth, as demonstrated by increasing site views and new users: A number of Information Providers were able to provide estimates of recent site statistics during the interview, expressing varying degrees of satisfaction with the numbers they are seeing. The general tone, however, was one of optimism: "[W]e know that we're at just under . . . 168,000 unique views in the last year. So . . . the fact that we know that 65 percent of those are first time meaning that we're . . . getting growth, we're getting lots of new folks."
2. An understanding of what users are looking for on the site (e.g., most popular topics) and how long they spend looking for it: In the words of one Information Provider, "we do keep track and look at first off, what's the primary search when people come to the site and what are the top landing pages? It's typically . . . an organic search—like Google or Bing or Yahoo!—people looking for divorce forms or something like that. So that's why they're highlighted. We also look at, you know, the number of people who land on those pages and how long they spend there." In the process of examining site usage data, Information Providers can make unexpected findings—one study participant described how Google Analytics helped her identify that certain groups of LEP individuals appear to have distinct information needs. For these individuals, she observed, the most frequently visited pages were not in the area of domestic relations/family law (the most popular content overall) but rather employment.
3. An understanding of how users are finding the site: An increase in the number of users coming to the site via search engines was observed by several study participants. One Information Provider explained that "it's now at about 76 percent of all visits come via search engines, whereas even as recently as early 2012, it was more like 55 percent. So . . . that's shaped my view about . . . how useful it is to obsess over the real estate of the front page. Nobody starts at the front page anymore. Three out of four people get there by doing a search for 'divorce' [in this state]."
4. The type of device they are using to access the site (e.g., desktop, laptop, tablet, smartphone): The growth in mobile access is of particular interest to Information Providers. As one study participant noted, "one of the things that Google Analytics shows [is] that we have 20-some percent accessing the site using smartphones."

Several Information Providers indicated that analytics aid them in making content-related decisions; however, one individual noted the limited nature of the information provided by usage statistics: "I think there's probably a lot more out there that we don't know. So, I use Google Analytics but . . . that's just measuring the people that are coming to the site so I don't know what people who don't even know about the site are [doing]."

The second evaluation effort discussed most frequently—the solicitation of user feedback—encompasses a variety of mechanisms that Information Providers use to obtain information directly from users, including online surveys, online feedback forms, focus groups, usability testing, e-mail/personal discussion, and outreach workshops.

- Online surveys: "[W]e use Survey Monkey. . . . I think it's at the end of our online application, and the response rate is just phenomenal because it pops up right after people finish submitting the application. So we have like an . . . 80 to 90 percent response rate. One of the questions is about income and household size and so we get all of that data about our users."
- Online feedback forms: "We also have a feedback form on our site and that's used quite heavily—most of the time it's people searching for legal information or advice but, even from those . . . e-mails, we're gleaning a lot of information about resources that, you know—maybe somebody is asking for a resource that we don't have and we need to build. Or they might be asking for a resource that we do have and then that can maybe clue us into the fact that we need to rename the resource because they didn't find it. Or they have a question that shows us that a certain piece of content is confusing and we need to revise it."
- Focus groups: "We have just started doing focus groups, which is not something that we ever tried to do as an organization. We just had our first one last month and we'll do another one this month . . . we started with a group of Spanish resources on the website [and] it was really an invaluable experience and that was, you know, seven people in a room facilitated by two of our staff people to talk about specific questions around resources . . . in Spanish."

Survey respondents were asked to provide examples of compliments, requests, and complaints they have received. As indicated by the sample of responses provided in table 5.3, users who take the time to provide feedback appear to be satisfied with the content that is available on the site (in particular, the forms) but would like to see more content that better meets their specific needs.

Users' requests for situation-specific information and for assistance directly from a person highlight their need for information that can assist them with a legal problem they are currently facing. One study participant, however, noted the difficulty in meeting this particular user need: "Each individual is looking for legal information specific to their issue and current situation. We have content in most areas that is general, but there is no way to create specific content for each unique situation."

Table 5.3. User Feedback (Sample Responses)

Complaints	*Requests*	*Compliments*
• Site needs more forms • Forms are not working • Unavailability of online intake for legal aid services • Available information does not apply to their individual situation • Browser incompatibility	• Information that is not currently covered on the website • Legal assistance/ representation • Better search capabilities	• Forms are useful • Instructions for forms make them easy to use • Information on site is easy to understand

Despite the fact that the provision of legal advice is outside the purview of statewide legal information websites, several survey respondents indicated that advice is precisely what some users are looking to receive through the website:

- "They wish they could talk to someone or ask a question."
- "Even though it clearly says we can't answer questions they think they can just e-mail in a question or can talk to someone on the website."
- "We get a lot of people telling us their whole life story, seeking help. They are looking for representation, but none is available."

Although the survey did not directly inquire about whether usability testing was conducted, respondents from two states did indicate that important feedback from users was obtained in this way. One respondent stated that usability testing was done during a recent redesign of the site, leading to a change "from a drill-down menu to a simple search engine based on usability testing." Another respondent made a reference to usability testing conducted during the early stages of the project, noting that this testing resulted in an improved user interface "to help those who are digital literacy challenged." The difficulty in finding target users who are willing to participate in usability testing or otherwise participate in website evaluation/design may be one reason why more states have not done it. This difficulty, as noted by the respondents from both of the states in which usability testing was conducted, also explains why intermediaries (e.g., legal aid attorneys, hotline staff) played such an important role in the identification of user needs during the development phase—they acted as a proxy for the actual target users who could not be reached.

The two Information Providers who mentioned usability testing in their survey responses were asked to discuss their experiences in more detail.[3] Both spoke with enthusiasm about what they learned throughout the process, with one describing how the testing they conducted in collaboration with a human-computer interaction class at a nearby iSchool led them to fundamentally redesign the home page. That result, as explained by the other Information Provider, is why usability testing is such a valuable endeavor:

> [U]sability testing always breaks down the functions that you go into. And that's why it's important to do, right, because you think one way is better and then you test it and realize that nobody understood that that's where the button was or what that word or phrase meant, what they were supposed to do next. So, yeah, I would say there's always . . . something that is learned from usability testing. You know, that's why it's so invaluable at this point. We need to do a better job of it . . . [make it] a part of our regular business process."

In addition to the feedback mechanisms listed above, several Information Providers noted the value of anecdotal evidence, which is often obtained through informal conversations with staff at other access to justice stakeholder organizations or clients of legal services providers. One Information Provider relayed the following story of how anecdotal evidence led to new content development:

> The other thing is just a single anecdote of going into the . . . circuit court, stopping in at—they have a little room there when you go in, it's like the self-help center or something like that—there's a paralegal behind the desk who said . . . "You know what we could really use? We could really use a page that talks about motions—like what a motion is. People have to file motions and they don't know what that means." And so . . . quickly we just put together a page on how to file a motion in circuit court and tried to really use—we had some of those best practices for clear writing in there in terms of interrogative question headings and the little picture of a caption to sort of show what a caption looks like. And then sort of a process view and things like that.

Although the majority of study participants indicated that they received feedback from some combination of the mechanisms described here (as well as others, including direct e-mail, LHI interviews, and online intake systems), there was no consensus as to how this feedback was handled and the extent to which it was acted upon.

Outreach

Interviewees were asked to talk about what they have done to make the website's presence known to the target audience and also to offer an opinion as to whether their efforts to date have been successful. As an initial matter, a number of Information Providers suggested that they are not doing as much outreach as they would like to do. As one interviewee observed,

> I would say that we have not done as much work with client groups and interest groups that, you know, see our clients and that would be natural sort of allies . . . at least with regard to the website. Now, I have to be careful because . . . we do work with interest groups and client groups with other stuff that we do, but not necessarily for website content. So, I think that, you know, that's kind of the thing that I would like to spend more time doing—going to client groups, just spending time with executive directors and groups of other . . . non-profits that work with our client population.

Because outreach activities are dependent on available resources and resource levels vary from state to state, many differences among states were observed. On one end of the spectrum are two states in which outreach has been institutionalized through a network of self-help centers in courts and libraries, one of which has gone a step further through the creation of a dedicated outreach coordinator to oversee this network. Part of the outreach coordinator's job is to maintain regular communication with the self-help centers through site visits and via a listserv, keeping everyone up to date on new content and features, important changes to the law, and any technology issues (e.g., scheduled website outages).

Other Information Providers use an array of outreach efforts to increase awareness about their statewide legal information websites. While some states have created print materials (e.g., brochures, posters) and other tangible items (e.g., magnets, pens) specifically for the website, others have folded outreach for the site into the organization's broader outreach activities:

- "[B]asically we include [statewide legal information website] information in every outreach activity that we do so we have business cards that have [the website URL] on one side and then on the other side is our helpline number. . . . So, yeah, for instance . . . we're going to . . . take a box of those cards and pass them out not only to the people who are there to access the services [at the veterans' organization] but also to other partners, community social services agency type folks. . . . Every . . . kind of outreach, kind of mailing that we do—like we're doing a low-income taxpayer clinic mailing across the state, we'll include information about [the website]. So, it's basically integrated into all of our outreach efforts."
- "Also, our staff do a lot of community outreach so they take . . . business cards that have our website address on them and other flyers to promote use of the website."

In addition to the distribution of promotional materials, Information Providers also use e-mail and social media—generally targeted to access to justice stakeholder organizations—to increase awareness about the site and promote recent changes.

LOOKING TO THE FUTURE: GREATER INTEGRATION OF LEGAL SERVICES

At the close of the interview, Information Providers were asked to talk about (1) the projects they were currently working on (see table 5.2), and (2) what they would most like to do in the future, if funding or staffing did not pose an issue. Several interviewees spoke about their plans to add content in certain areas in which they are seeing more demand (e.g., consumer debt collection, unemployment). In a number of interviews, however, it became clear that the changes that Information Providers most want to see (and in many cases were already working on) did not involve minor modifications to site content but rather a reenvisioning of the role that statewide legal information websites are to play in the delivery of legal services in the future. As one Pro Bono Net staff member explained, in an increasing number of states, "it's no longer just about 'Hey! We're delivering, you know, [information about] your rights.' It's 'come here to get access to . . . more of like a virtual services model.'" The idea of creating a more interactive experience embodied in many of the projects discussed in table 5.2 evidences a problem-solving approach: "[I]nstead of just [providing] a long list of keywords or a search box, trying to ask questions—what did you come here for? What's your specific need? Let's narrow that down—is it one of these three choices? So, it's a simple, you know, logic system or a triage system and you try to specifically generate content for them based on the unique individual." Further development of online forms is seen by some Information Providers as a necessary step toward transforming websites into problem-solving tools. One interviewee observed that "[i]t's all fine and good to have a tutorial about what a divorce is all about but I want the person to be able to go from that legal information phase into a legal action phase, to be able to create their own forms—print them, file them, and then have a good outcome in their case."

Information Providers described this idea of integrating the statewide legal information website into the broader legal services system in different ways. But a common thread among Information Providers' visions of integrated legal services was the capacity to usher people through the necessary legal processes and procedures by providing more streamlined content. One Information Provider, who is currently building an online triage system, described a scenario in which a website visitor could access relevant information before being transferred to the intake unit. At that point, the user's data would be entered into the case management system as well. The integration of these systems, he surmised, should ease the transition from website user to applicant to client. Similarly, a Pro Bono Net staff member described a current project that involves connecting API content feeds from websites with case management systems at legal services organizations. The result of building these bridges between currently separate systems could be something like this:

> [S]omebody who's on the phone with a hotline worker or an advocate who's on the phone with somebody who's being evicted, can be entering their record in the case management system for them and setting up. . . . a legal services appointment, [while] at the same time, pulling in through that record, like a set of . . . the top three eviction resources on the [website] and being able to quickly say, "Hey, I'm going to send you links to three booklets for your appointment."

For others, the idea of integrated services means developing a better understanding of how people's legal needs intersect with other needs: "[W]hen someone has a civil legal problem, it's a real driver for them to find help of all kinds and so . . . it sort of made sense for us to . . . combine the social services issues with the legal problems so we sort of tried to broaden what we include on the site to include those links to social service resources."

It is important to recognize that, in states with particularly challenging environments, many of the projects described in table 5.2 are aspirational. Triage systems and a streamlined process for filing online forms, for example, are still "wish list" items for some Information Providers. Other interviewees talked about how they would like to add more interactive features to the site ("I'd like to come up with something . . . like an Angie's List for poor people in terms of resources"); incorporate more multimedia resources ("I'd like to add more video resources on there because I think a lot of times no matter how clear we think we've been on the text, a lot of clients with low literacy levels or other barriers have a hard time absorbing anything beyond more than, you know, a few paragraphs"); conduct additional outreach efforts ("I'd also like to connect with the adult education department . . . in the government at the state level and see if there is a way that we can work our website into their curriculum"); or use the website as a means to promote in-person legal clinics hosted by other organizations.

As the foregoing discussion demonstrates, Information Providers approach each of the four principal program activities—content development and review, website design, outreach, and evaluation—with the goal of delivering website content that connects self-help users with the legal information and services they seek. To date, they have struggled with achieving this goal. Information Providers are routinely confronted by challenges created by limited budgets and staffing, while also facing resistance from stakeholders who fail to understand or appreciate how the website provides assistance to self-help users. Thus, while they recognize that they have yet to successfully overcome all of the barriers to information access created by language and literacy, many Information Providers currently lack the capacity to turn their ideas about overcoming these barriers into action items. The silver lining described by many study participants, however, is the collaborative efforts they have undertaken with other access to justice stakeholders, as well as with other Information Providers. As discussed in greater detail in chapter 6, collaboration is a key component to better integrating statewide legal information websites with other legal services. Moreover, it may in fact be the solution to one of the most significant problems facing Information Providers that came to light during this study—their lack of connection with the users of statewide legal information websites.

NOTES

1. The State Justice Institute "award[s] grants to improve the quality of justice in State courts, facilitate better coordination between State and Federal courts, and foster innovative, efficient solutions to common issues faced by all courts" (State Justice Institute, n.d.).

2. According to the National Legal Aid and Defender Association (NLADA), "[t]he Reagan Administration was openly hostile to legal services and initially sought its complete elimination. . . . In response to pressure from the White House, Congress reduced funding for

[LSC] for 1982 by 25%. . . . [T]his reduction[] coincided with a national economic recession and a marked reduction . . . in programs affecting poor people, substantially increasing the eligible population and the demand for legal services" (NLADA, n.d.).

3. This is not to say that the other websites have not undergone usability testing. Per a Pro Bono Net staff member, user testing was done during the development of LH3, the latest iteration of the LawHelp platform.

6

Collaboration in the Realm of Access to Justice

A cursory glance at many statewide legal information websites fails to reveal the collaboration underlying them. In fact, the websites typically appear to be the work of one organization (most often a provider of legal services), and it is necessary to do a little digging into the site to get a clearer sense of how other organizations have contributed, in one way or another, to the finished product. The initial literature review conducted for this study, however, provided some hints that collaboration was a driving force behind many of these websites. Zorza (2010), for example, described how LawHelp NY works closely with the court system in posting information and also provides training to the staff of public and law libraries. The goal of this training is to leverage librarians' experience in conducting outreach to populations who may not be aware of available legal resources (e.g., individuals with LEP). Collaboration can also be seen in projects that deploy document assembly software to make court forms available online. For example, in a number of states (e.g., Idaho, New York, Vermont), online forms developed by the state court system have been loaded into LHI, a component of many statewide legal information websites.

This phenomenon was explored through both the survey and the interviews, where differences in terms of the nature and extent of this collaboration came to light. At the broadest level, two forms of collaboration were documented: cooperation among Information Providers in different states and cooperation among organizations that comprise the access to justice community within a state.

COLLABORATION AMONG STATES

As described by one Pro Bono Net staff member, the community of Information Providers is diverse, comprised of a mixture of people who "love technology for technology's sake" and people who view technology as a means to provide better services to clients. These two groups balance each other out, with the former group encouraging innovation and the latter group ensuring that the focus remains on the users.

As Information Providers struggle with budget, staffing, and other operational issues, they look to see how their counterparts in other states are faring. Such efforts are guided by several organizations that facilitate knowledge sharing and learning among this community. LSC continues to support the growth of statewide legal information websites, notwithstanding its diminished funding role in recent years. As described by one study participant, LSC has "been useful in terms of [being] a sounding board and keeping us in touch with other programs who are also developing websites or changing websites and . . . they've created a forum for discussion of the whole and they certainly have been encouraging innovation around the websites." LSC also holds an annual TIG conference that facilitates an ongoing dialogue about many of the issues identified in this study. Last year's conference, for example, included sessions focused on online triage and intake, as well as other interactive features (e.g., online forms) that increasingly serve as integral components of statewide legal information websites.

Moreover, the LawHelp and OST communities both provide ample opportunities for Information Providers to share their experiences and innovations so that they do not have to reinvent the proverbial wheel. Several study participants detailed how Pro Bono Net was a key driving force behind early collaboration efforts that laid the foundation for the strong ties that exist among Information Providers today. The Circuit Rider program,[1] for example, was instrumental in helping a sense of community among LawHelp states to emerge. Pro Bono Net developed this program through a TIG received by the Northwest Justice Project (in Washington State) to provide project assistance to statewide legal information websites using the LawHelp platform. As described in a 2007 report (the "Circuit Rider Report"),

> Circuit Riders help state justice communities understand how to take full advantage of their template software, to generate and maintain legal content, to involve and work with a wide array of community stakeholders, to market their sites, and to evaluate their sites' effectiveness. Circuit Riders also develop resource materials, facilitate regular meetings among state partners, make site visits to problem-solve project issues, and conduct outreach to diverse audiences. They also serve as a link between statewide website efforts in different states, allowing website developers to tap into and learn from similar efforts elsewhere. (Weber, 2007, p. 9)

Circuit riders facilitated interstate communication through a variety of means, including in-person visits, remote assistance (via e-mail and the telephone), monthly teleconferences, and a listserv. Although the Circuit Rider program has been disbanded, the sense of community among LawHelp states remains strong. Several Information Providers from LawHelp states described the benefits they reap by virtue of being part of this network:

- "We have a sense of community with the other LawHelp states—whenever we're looking at things we want to do to improve our websites, we don't have to look far because, you know, there are people all along the spectrum, in terms of where they are in their development and . . . they're willing to help and you know help each other out. And then of course I can't forget to mention the Pro Bono Net staff, the LawHelp staff—it's just really tremendous to have experts on call. . . . It's just great to know that if I have a question or I have a feature request or I have an idea or I need support, it's just an e-mail or phone call away. It's just truly incredible."
- "[B]asically, any time we have a question or . . . we're looking for a way to do something particular, we can reach out to anyone we know basically who [is] maintaining [a] LawHelp website and get that help. Everybody is very forthcoming in sharing tricks and tips and information and content, which is amazing. . . . I've never felt that I couldn't reach out to a coordinator even if I didn't know him or her and have a good response. And I think that we do benefit from the acquired knowledge from the group, you know, certain LawHelps will try one thing and either succeed or fail and be very open about that and so we can kind of learn, you know, without doing."

It should be noted that, in addition to developing the LawHelp platform, Pro Bono Net has also been involved in a variety of community events and grant-funded projects that have benefited the entire network of statewide legal information websites. It has partnered with LawHelp states as well as those on other platforms to develop new features and tools (e.g., online triage, text-based information referral services). In addition, since 2014, Pro Bono Net, in conjunction with the Legal Services National Technology Assistance Project (LSNTAP), has been running a webinar series "for all stakeholders involved in legal services technology and maximizing the delivery of services to clients." The first webinar in 2016 focused on technology tips, emphasizing "homegrown" tools and resources developed by legal services providers. A subsequent webinar explored outcomes evaluation and the ways in which approaches commonly used in other fields can be applied within the context of legal services.

Although the OST network is less formal than that created by Pro Bono Net, Information Providers in that group have also developed various means to connect with one another, including meetings at TIG annual conferences, a listserv, and conference calls. In the early 2000s, LSNTAP developed a circuit rider program for the OST community, similar to that described above for LawHelp states. More recently, as described by one Information Provider, through collaboration, a group of Information Providers within this community has joined forces to secure grant funds to create an updated open source template:

> [I]n [an earlier grant], we wrote into the milestones, that we would have monthly meetings, tele-meetings or webinars or go-to-meeting type things—get people in [the OST]

> community involved and brainstorming and decision-making and just up to date and so I guess the infrastructure of the group, the community was already in place. We just leveraged what was already happening and started having more frequent meetings via telephone and computer and since we ended up writing the first grant, it just fell on us to continue the follow-up grants to build more, to update the template, and so on and so forth. And now we're on our . . . fourth Drupal grant. [W]e . . . don't have the meetings on a monthly basis anymore but we do have them about once a quarter to update people. But, there [are] . . . e-mails and phone calls going out back and forth and, at this point, we're just trying to find people out there that, either didn't move their website from one platform to the newest or went out on their own and now just kind of have an old Titanic iceberg floating out there that they need to update.

This quote emphasizes the inclusive nature of the community of Information Providers. Notwithstanding differences in platform, there is a prevailing sense that they can learn from, as well as offer assistance to, one another. This collaboration among Information Providers can offset, at least to some extent, a tense environment within one's own legal services community.

COLLABORATION WITHIN STATES

Just as the broader environment in which each website is situated has shaped their development and implementation, it has also impacted the ways in which Information Providers work with other access to justice stakeholders within the state. Legal services organizations (both direct service providers and statewide support organizations), courts, libraries (generally public libraries and public law libraries), and law schools were all identified by a number of study participants as key partners. Domestic violence survivor shelters and advocacy organizations, colleges and universities, and technology centers were also named as collaborators, albeit by a smaller number of study participants. The work of this latter group of organizations, in particular, raises important questions about the contributions that less "traditional" access to justice stakeholders can make to statewide legal information websites and related initiatives.

In many states, collaboration appears to have been part of the equation from the very beginning of project development. Although other legal aid organizations were most frequently named as initial collaborators, other groups that took on an early role include family law self-help centers, pro bono programs, law schools, state courts, state bars, law libraries, private attorneys, and access to justice bodies. One study participant, for example, noted that "[a] group of stakeholders from legal aid, law school, and funding communities engaged in a planning session to determine the scope of information to be initially included on the site."

Other Information Providers discussed how, during the early stages of developing their sites, they needed to reach out to other organizations to ensure that there was enough content on the site when it launched. As described by one study participant, after inventorying the materials available on other statewide legal information websites, she concluded that she lacked sufficient resources to develop enough valuable content on her own. She was fortunate, however, because one legal services organization in the state had a strong community education department, which had developed and already made available online a large library of newsletters, handouts, articles, and other materials written specifically for clients. With the assistance of this organization, as well as others, the statewide legal information website was populated in a timely manner with a variety of materials on important topics.

This collaborative spirit remains strong today—the majority of survey respondents indicated that they maintain working relationships with state and local bar associations, law schools within the state, and other legal services projects/programs within the state. The ways in which other organizations play an active role with respect to the sites varies widely and, through the study, it became clear that contributions by other organizations impact the websites at different levels—their day-to-day operations as well as their strategic directions. Table 6.1 lays out the different roles that access to justice stakeholder organizations play in connection with statewide legal information websites.

Discussions with Information Providers about these different roles revealed a fair amount of variation in terms of the extent to which collaboration is formalized. Advisory committees are one vehicle for providing collaborative ventures with a structure. For example, in one state, the website stakeholder committee, which meets three times a year, consists of members from the eight largest legal-aid organizations in the state. This state also has an advisory committee for its Spanish-language site comprised of members from various legal services organizations that work with the Latino population. Overall, Information Providers representing five states indicated that they currently have an advisory committee specifically for the website, whereas several Information Providers indicated that earlier efforts to maintain an advisory committee had fallen to the wayside. Information Providers from three of the states that currently maintain advisory committees emphasized the diversity of committee membership:

- "[W]e have people from . . . each legal aid organization, our major bar foundation funder, people at different law schools, and social services organizations that work directly with our client populations, and also technical people from our legal aid organizations."
- "[W]e have . . . a representative from the state bar. We have several judges. We have a couple of people from legal services organizations. We have a couple of people from self-help centers. We have a couple of people from the state court administrative office and someone from the [state] Judicial Institute and . . . someone from the state bar foundation."
- "Well, we originally had a librarian—we had sort of the director of the regional library, one library director, one of our IT people. We've got a few of those information people that tend to do community education for legal aid programs. We have someone from the administrative office of the courts."

Table 6.1. Roles of Access to Justice Stakeholder Organizations[1]

	Content Development	*Funder*	*Host of Legal Clinic/Self-Help Center*	*Outreach[2]*	*Participation in Advisory Committee*	*Provider of Self-Help Resources*	*Provider of Feedback*	*LiveHelp Navigators*
Access to justice commission	1			1	1	1	2	
Advocacy groups	1			2				
Bar associations	3			2	1		2	
Bar foundations		5		1	2			
Colleges/universities	3							
Courts	3		2	10	3	1	4	
DV shelters/orgs	1			4	1		2	
Gov't agencies	2	2		2	1	1	2	
Law schools	8				2	1	1	2
Legal services organizations	19			5	5		2	
Libraries	1		3	14	2		3	
Non-profit organizations	2	1		6	3		2	
Places of worship				2				
Private bar	1	1		3				
Pro bono community	6						1	
Self-help centers				2	1		1	
Self-help task forces							1	
Senior centers				1				
Social services agencies				4	2		1	
State bar	1			2	2		1	
State legislature				1				
Technology centers			1	1				

[1] The number in each box represents the number of states in which a particular type of organization fulfills that particular role.

[2] Outreach includes trainings and other activities by Information Providers to increase awareness about the site among access to justice stakeholder organizations, as well as the stakeholder organizations' efforts to disseminate information about the site.

The role of advisory committees varies, with one Information Provider describing its duties as broad oversight (noting that many members are executive directors of legal services and other non-profit organizations and therefore lack the time to "micromanage") and others indicating a more active role for the committee:

> [T]he role of the stakeholder committee is really to guide our programmatic priorities and to . . . engage them in the work of the websites. And so . . . we often use them as, as sort of our first point of contact for when we're looking to update a piece of content, right? So, we send [it] out and say, "We need to update this content on how to get custody of a child," for example. And, folks will respond to us with their suggestions from their respective organizations.

As with content development and other work associated with the websites, however, it can be challenging to maintain a high level of involvement across the entire committee, and some members will inevitably remain more engaged than others.

In other states, Information Providers' collaborative efforts with other organizations were more or less ad hoc from the beginning. In discussing their relationships with access to justice stakeholder organizations, several Information Providers described how they maintain open channels of communications through which informal conversations about the needs of self-help users and other potential site users occur. These ongoing conversations have minimized the need for formal structures to facilitate cooperation. As noted by one study participant, the decision not to have an advisory committee specifically for the website was due to solid existing relationships with the organizations with which they were most likely to collaborate:

> [M]any of our interested stakeholders are involved with us in other committees and commissions. For instance, [the] access to justice commission, self-represented litigants committees, etc. So, generally, all of the input about [the website] generally comes out during those meetings. As well as . . . we just have great weekly, if not daily, dealings with our state bar, our law library, other access to justice folks, so just those conversations happen really naturally. . . . [S]o, basically we felt that trying to have a stakeholders meeting once every quarter or whatnot was overkill—it wasn't necessary. It was happening already in other forums.

Moreover, regardless of the nature of the collaborative relationship, waning involvement and enthusiasm is an issue with which many Information Providers contend. As with content development, lack of time and resources can impede collaborative efforts, as government agencies and non-profit organizations have been impacted by broader economic forces as well. An additional challenge noted was staff turnover within partner organizations. One Information Provider, who had cultivated a relationship with staff members at the state department of health and human services and was working with them to avoid posting duplicative information, described how management changes in that department slowed progress as the new leaders did not understand the process in place. Yet another challenge noted was the existence of divergent interests among stakeholder groups, which can lead to differing opinions as to the proper scope, purpose, and future directions of the site. By way of example, one Information Provider noted that, as members of the private bar struggle to make a living, they are less inclined to champion self-help resources aimed at their potential clients:

> And so, right now, the trial lawyers are hurting real bad because the Republicans have taken over the statehouse and the state senate and the governor. So, one of the first things that happened was that the pro-business strategy by the new government, the new administration, was to totally revamp worker's comp and trial lawyers—that's always been their bread and butter—it's gone, you know. There's still a system but the stream of income is gone, so they're all looking around for a new practice area. . . . [B]ut the reality is that the idea that people will be doing their own divorces, custody, they're not happy with this. So I don't know what the court is hearing from that, but they're not cooperative on the ground in my area.

In some cases, interests among access to justice stakeholder organizations have diverged to the point that collaboration is not feasible. The friction among legal services providers described by several study participants stands in stark contrast to those Information Providers who described generally amicable relationships within this community. One individual explained that

> if you have a good working relationship, you know, California from the get-go was working closely with their court system . . . [but] there's a lot of animus between pretty much everyone and our program, so there wasn't a real likelihood—the state ended up funding pro bono in the most unique way, largely in part so that the funds did not get to come to our program. . . . [This] is an extremely, extremely conservative state that frowns upon federal funding for anything—one of our peer legal service programs . . . within the first three sentences of its promotional stuff says "we're not federally funded."

Among those who expressed the greatest discontent with their current situations, the underlying problems varied. One study participant noted that her organization was the only legal services provider in the entire state, whereas others had a distant (and, in one case, contentious) relationship with other legal services organizations in the state. In the latter cases, the Information Providers expressed skepticism about the value of building stakeholder relationships. A Pro Bono Net staff member offered the following frank assessment of the situation in some states:

> "[It] is all based on local resources. . . . So, if you don't have a good relationship with the bar, if you don't have a good relationship with the courts, if your courts don't care or believe that self-help resources make sense, how are you going to create the network to allow these people to proceed to court on their own? So, it takes a village, you know, to get the person through. In some states, that's been done well. And, in other states, it is, you know, an evolving process. Rome was not built in one day and we're building Rome.

She described, for example, how the success of online forms projects varies from state to state, often depending on the extent to which history and politics prevents groups from being flexible with their demands and willing to trust one another.

Even organizations that work together well can have conflicting interests. Some courts' reluctance to embrace the use of automated forms is one example of this type of conflict. Several Information Providers indicated that the courts' stance was a significant impediment to progress in this area, citing it as a primary reason for their decision not to include a full suite of online forms on their websites. Cooperation is particularly important in this context, though, as the court is the ultimate arbiter of whether a given form will be accepted.

Moreover, many access to justice stakeholders are supportive of statewide legal information websites in theory but appear to be shying away from playing a more active role. One Information Provider's description of the library community's lukewarm involvement in the site aptly illustrates this point: "[W]e really urged them [librarians] to participate in the trainings and have a presence on our site and very few of them really took initiative to do that. They use the resource but they really didn't see why they should care about having a presence on our site."

In some states, for example, working on the website is promoted as a way for attorneys to fulfill their pro bono hours. Several Information Providers, however, report that attorneys tend to gravitate toward direct client services for their pro bono hours, feeling that it is a more valuable form of volunteer service. Repeated unsuccessful efforts to gain traction within the legal services community have left several Information Providers feeling discouraged. They have good ideas, such as one study participant's earlier outreach efforts focused on low-income teenagers based on her belief that teenagers are likely to be the ones going online to search for information needed by other family members. But Information Providers' inability to gain support for their ideas—from those within their organizations as well as within the broader access to justice community—creates an impasse that they do not know how to overcome.

This impasse is even more problematic in light of ongoing efforts to build online intake and triage systems that are integrated with statewide legal information websites. A number of study participants suggested that some members of the legal services community are not ready to make this leap to a system that encompasses both in-person and virtual services. As one Pro Bono Net staff member noted, "Even phone intake is in some places disparaged, right? So this notion of changing the way we practice law and how we provide services, not everybody is there yet."

These difficulties appear to stem, at least in part, from the fractionalized nature of the legal services community in some states. In some states, there is more than one website that provides information for self-help users. Cooperation among the various access to justice stakeholders that maintain these sites (notably, courts, libraries, and legal services organizations) has been one way to streamline efforts. One Information Provider described how the high level of collaboration among legal services providers in their state increases efficiency: "[W]e've made a big push . . . with all of the different organizations creating web resources to try to not duplicate effort so that we can maximize the use of the staff and the money that we have. So we've actually created an inventory of resources that people can access to look at before they decide to develop a resource."

This is not necessarily the norm, however. As one Pro Bono Net staff member described, there is not always integration between the statewide legal information website and the online resources other organizations are creating for self-help users. The reasons for this lack of cohesiveness, ranging from the lack of a statewide technology support group to a history of tension between legal services organizations, were touched upon during interviews, but a thorough exploration of these reasons was beyond the scope of the current study. Regardless of the reason, a fractionalized system is problematic within a statewide legal information context to the extent that it leads to duplication of effort. Moreover, it does a disservice to self-help users as they have to move from site to site to obtain the various information resources and services they need. The solution, according to one Information Provider, is the development of online portals that bring together multimedia resources, forms, content written pursuant to the principles of plain language, and chat services all in one place. This solution, it is worth noting, closely resembles the proposal that emerged from the LSC summit. While there is progress being made in this area, there are still far too many stand-alone websites, the existence of which detracts from efforts to convince members of the legal services community to focus their efforts specifically on the statewide legal information website. As a result, many Information Providers find themselves unable to pull together a committed corps of individuals who are invested enough in the site to contribute to it on a regular basis.

Information Providers working in states with fractionalized systems talked about the lack of a shared vision and the role of the access to justice commission (or similar statewide entity) in remedying this situation. In other states, it appears as if the access to justice commission has been instrumental in bringing awareness to self-represented litigants and has embraced the statewide legal information website as a central part of efforts to better serve this population. One Information Provider, however, painted a bleaker portrait, explaining how the vision of the access to justice commission in her state conceives of the needs of self-help users in a way that does not quite mesh with the mission of the statewide legal information website. She offered the following example to illustrate this point: "[A] lot of the content that we might develop might be how to represent yourself in a [Medicaid] hearing. Well, that doesn't help the commission at all because they don't care what happens in administrative hearings. They only care about what happens in the public court system."

Despite these concerns about the lack of cohesiveness within the access to justice community, this study brought to light emerging partnerships with non-traditional access to justice stakeholder organizations (e.g., technology centers, places of worship) as well as emerging roles and responsibilities within existing partnerships. For example, as reflected in table 6.1, legal services providers, law schools, and the pro bono community are the most frequent contributors to content development, in line with Information Providers' interest in having substantive experts involved in this process. Examples of collaborative efforts described by study participants include the following: (1) interactive forms and materials for specific populations, such as domestic violence survivors; (2) translated materials for mirror sites; (3) the development of videos and other multimedia resources; and (4) the transcription of videos and archived webinars. Such collaborative efforts with "likeminded organizations" can be grant driven. In fact, several Information Providers suggested that LSC grantee organizations have an obligation to contribute to the website, with one asserting that specific grant assurances create this obligation.[2]

One particularly interesting collaborative effort described by a study participant involves a law school brief advice clinic—the Information Provider provides clear-writing training to the students, they draft content for the website, and he continues to work with them on incorporating clear writing principles through several rounds of drafts before a substantive expert weighs in. This particular Information Provider has also started offering clear writing training to summer interns at legal services organizations. These efforts, he explained, serve various purposes, namely, community service, marketing, and "preparation for getting people involved" in the website as they start their legal careers. Others are also increasingly thinking about the role that law students can play. Another study participant, for example, is currently developing a project that would work the website into the curriculum of adult education (including English as second language) classes. The Information Provider envisions law students conducting these presentations and thus playing a central role in this outreach effort.

While providers of legal services are most likely to help with content development, courts, libraries, and non-profit organizations play an equally important role by engaging in outreach activities targeted at increasing awareness about the site. Information Providers often send out regular communications to libraries, advocacy groups, community action groups, social services agencies, and other outreach partners about new content or other site updates, with the hope that they pass this information along to the public. One study participant, for example, stated that various partners distribute promotional materials for the website (e.g., flyers, brochures, business cards), and other study participants noted the value of having other organizations posting links to the website on their own site.

A number of Information Providers, however, have engaged in more concerted outreach activities. These efforts include giving presentations about the website (and other related initiatives) at conferences attended by access to justice stakeholder organizations and holding in-person and online training sessions. As the following quotes demonstrate, training sessions for libraries are common, but several Information Providers also offered examples of outreach to other organizations that can benefit from learning more about the websites:

- "I went and did a training to legislative staff. I'm actually a registered lobbyist for our organization—I know a lot of people down at the hill. So, I did a training for the legislative staff and that went over really well."

- "And we had one staff member go to their local libraries and talk to the librarians about our website, and specifically the interactive court forms for those who can't afford a lawyer. And so they were given that information, and the same is true about a lot of the shelters and the other advocacy groups, they were given some training on those."
- "And so in that process of . . . planning and opening the legal self-help centers, we do trainings for the librarians, the circuit clerks, anyone on the court staff who is interested and anyone else in the community who wants to come, basically."
- "I got together with the state library . . . which is sort of the umbrella group for all of the public libraries in the state to present. We did two things—we did a webinar series for librarians [across the state], and we also went on a road show and did in-person trainings about the legal resources available online, including of course . . . our website."

FOSTERING STRONGER TIES

These outreach efforts laid the foundation for deeper collaborative efforts aimed at connecting people with the legal information they need through statewide legal information websites. The partnerships between the legal services and library communities currently emerging are of particular interest. As described by one study participant, "[L]ibraries are seen as kind of natural places where people come to get information and help from a librarian. You can get free Internet there—so they [are] just natural community hubs."

Evidence of the expanded role of libraries and librarians in the access to justice movement can be seen in the increasing number of librarians from public law libraries serving on statewide access to justice commissions in a number of states, including California, Illinois, Kentucky, Maryland, Massachusetts, Montana, New Mexico, Texas, and Washington. Moreover, librarians' voices increasingly help to shape statewide legal information websites. As observed by Ledray (2013), librarians are often able to provide feedback on the usefulness of the site in terms of both content and design.

And, in fact, libraries were front and center during the development of one statewide legal information website, which was expressly designed to aid librarians in their intermediary role. Prior to developing the site, a legal services organization within the state conducted a survey to assess librarians' needs related to the provision of legal information. Through this survey, they learned that many librarians did not feel qualified to answer the legal questions they were being asked, despite having received some training on how to distinguish between legal advice and legal information. In addition to incorporating resources specifically for librarians into the site, the Information Providers have conducted numerous trainings with librarians throughout the state. This continues today on a smaller scale (by phone and one-on-one sessions), as they train new librarians and offer refresher courses. One study participant noted that librarians' responses to the site have been generally positive. In one library where they hold monthly pro bono clinics in conjunction with a local legal services organization, the librarians "have been ape" over the website because it is a resource to which they can point patrons who come in with legal questions throughout the month.

Other notable examples of collaboration related to statewide legal information websites include the following:

- The Travis County Law Library (Texas) worked with the judges and the clerk of the court to develop a set of locally approved court forms that are now available on TexasLawHelp.org (Fritschel, 2007).
- Many of the technology-based legal self-help centers established by Illinois Legal Aid Online, a non-profit organization that emerged out of a collaboration among Chicago-Kent College of Law, the Chicago Bar Foundation, and the Lawyers Trust Fund, are located in public libraries (Zorza, 2010).
- Central Minnesota Legal Services received a grant from LSC to develop library–legal aid collaborations, including a statewide webinar series to train librarians on online legal resources.

These initiatives all bring to mind the concept of scaffolding, which was explored by Bishop, Tidline, Shoemaker, and Salela (1999) in the context of providing networked information services to disenfranchised groups. More recently, the 2014 Digital Inclusion Survey—a joint undertaking of the American Library Association and the Information Policy & Access Center at the University of Maryland—revealed the various ways that public libraries today offer a bridge to information and resources in a number of critical areas, including education, employment, health, and e-government/civic engagement (Bertot, Real, Lee, McDermott, & Jaeger, 2015). A few key statistics related to each of these areas will suffice to drive this point home:

Education: 94.3 percent of public libraries offer summer reading programs for children; 72.6 percent offer GED preparation assistance.

Employment: 62.3 percent offer access to subscription-based job training websites; 73.1 percent provide instruction in essential skills for job seekers (e.g., resume preparation, completion of online applications).

Health: 59 percent offer programs designed to help individuals identify health information resources; 48 percent offer programming focused on health and wellness topics.

E-government/civic engagement: 75.6 percent assist patrons with accessing and using e-government programs and services; 40.2 percent host community engagement events such as candidate conversations.

Within the realm of e-government in particular, we see how public libraries provide much-needed scaffolding, assisting patrons with the technology and civic literacy knowledge needed to access information and resources (Jaeger et al., 2015; Taylor, Gorham, Jaeger, & Bertot, 2014). Many public libraries have expanded beyond point-of-use services to implement programs that specifically address the range of skills needed to successfully engage in e-government activities. By way of example, over ten years ago, the U.S. Department of State mandated that the diversity visa application process be completed online. Recognizing the difficulty that this would pose for many members of the surrounding community, the Queens Library in New York (working with the Mayor's Office of Immigrant Affairs) set up designated times at different branches during which immigrants were able to receive assistance with scanning photographs to be submitted with their applications (Yaniv, 2005).

Moreover, in some cases, government agencies are becoming increasingly dependent on libraries fulfilling this role, with some even instructing website users to visit the local library if they need assistance related to the site (Jaeger & Bertot, 2011). Recently, implementation of the Affordable Care Act (ACA) highlighted the government's growing reliance on public libraries (Real, McDermott, Bertot, & Jaeger, 2015; Rembold, 2014). As noted by Real et al.,

> [u]nder the ACA, millions of people—perhaps tens of millions—were anticipated to sign up online for health insurance, and a great many of them were expected to depend on public library resources and services to do so. With 15 percent of American adults being nonusers of the Internet, much of the work with health care enrollment began with basic digital literacy education at the public library. In advance of the launch of the ACA enrollment site, the U.S. Department of Health and Human Services (DHHS) stated that it expected considerable support from public libraries to both inform people about options and help them enroll[.] (internal citations omitted)

There is no reason to believe that librarians cannot play a similar role with respect to connecting self-help users with the legal information and resources they need to navigate the legal system. Indeed, several study participants discussed the role of navigators in enhancing access to the services available through self-help centers, including access to statewide legal information websites. In essence, navigators are "people on the ground" who can guide self-represented litigants through the court system. For example, in Michigan, self-help centers located in courthouses and libraries typically are staffed with navigators "who can help visitors find what they need on the Michigan Legal Help website, answer questions about court practices and processes, and answer simple questions that are available on the website."

With navigators, all self-help users—even those who struggle with access to online legal information due to any number of barriers—can use the valuable information and resources available on statewide legal information websites. The growing use of navigators in this area is a testament to the collaborative spirit that is currently thriving within the access to justice community. We know, however, that this community is not complacent and is always looking for innovative ways to better serve individuals with unmet legal needs in this country. With that in mind, the final chapter opens up a dialogue about the different ways in which this collaborative spirit can be harnessed to enhance the services provided through statewide legal information websites and related initiatives.

NOTES

1. "Circuit-Riding is a term of art in the technology industry. It comes from 'riding the circuit,' or traveling on-site among various programs and providing in-depth assistance" (LSNTAP, n.d., "Definition of Circuit Riding").

2. This position appears to have merit. Pursuant to the 2014 LSC grant assurances, LSC grantee organizations "will work with other LSC and non-LSC funded legal services providers in the State to ensure that there is a statewide website that publishes a full range of relevant and up-to-date community education/pro se related materials and referral information, at least covering the common topics facing the client communities on the subject matter that are the [organization's] priorities."

7

Recommendations for Policy and Practice

In April 2014, Glenn Rawdon, LSC Technology Program counsel, gave an inspired speech at the White House Forum on Increasing Access to Justice. He began this speech with a reference to a 1999 article written by Bill Gates (titled "Everyone, Anytime, Anywhere") that described a time in the future when universal access would be achieved through the convergence of all the necessary parts—the people, the infrastructure, and the technology. As Rawdon noted, the Gates article was written around the time that the LSC was first funding projects through the TIG program. The hundreds of TIG projects developed since that time laid the very important foundation for using technology to promote access to justice; however, as a Pro Bono Net staff member interviewed for my dissertation study astutely observed, "[i]t's not just all about the technology." Convergence within the realm of access to justice is occurring at this point in time because of the people who are committed to making equal access to justice a reality rather than an aspiration: "Legal aid, the bench, the bar, law schools, libraries, and anyone else who cares about justice, coming together so all the pieces are there. No more each building our own systems, but a cooperative approach to provide the information, advice, and representation needed so that access to justice is there for Everyone, Anytime, Anywhere."

This sentiment is echoed in an article published in the 2015 edition of *Trends in State Courts* (an annual NCSC publication) that discusses the collaborative nature of PLL, the Maryland statewide legal information website that was the subject of my initial research in this area. This article, written by the site's current web content coordinator (Pantzer, 2016), details how the diverse perspective of legal and nonlegal professionals has contributed to the site's continual growth and improvement:

> Law librarians and legal-services attorneys (who deal with a steady stream of practical legal questions) identify topics for which the public needs better information. Law

> librarians and law-school clinical programs have the skills and resources to sketch out this new content identifying relevant laws, documents and information. The experience of practicing attorneys and the perspectives of government employees add additional layers of depth to the content. After content is written and edited, language students and bilingual attorneys and translators provide non-English versions. The Maryland State Law Library organizes and maintains the content and coordinates its ongoing review when the law changes. When new content becomes available, public libraries, court staff, and a variety of nonprofit organizations put it in the hands of the public. (pp. 62–63)

This quote, as well as Rawdon's speech, aptly captures the key theme discussed in the previous chapter, namely, how collaboration can enhance the development and dissemination of online legal information resources and services. Yet the impact of collaboration—that is, the extent to which website users benefit from it—remains an underexplored area. As explained in the introduction, LSC has adopted the position that statewide legal information websites can and should serve as platforms for integrated legal services delivery systems. They are deemed to be an integral part of future legal services, notwithstanding the fact that we are only beginning to understand how they facilitate access to legal information by those who most need it. Without continuing efforts to enhance this understanding, the LSC's carefully constructed vision could falter.

Also of concern is the fact that there is a mismatch between this vision and the current situation in many of the states from which data were collected. The survey and interviews revealed that these websites are not often seen as a priority by everyone within the organization that maintains them, leaving them vulnerable in the face of ongoing budgetary and staffing reductions. At the same time, the economic constraints permeating the legal services community have led to increasing calls for programs to justify their existence by demonstrating their effectiveness. Statewide legal information websites and related initiatives have not been immune to these calls, as Information Providers in many states still struggle to gain traction within their own organizations as well as in the broader legal services community.

Moreover, many Information Providers find themselves in a difficult position due to a lack of connection with their actual users that precludes them from demonstrating their effectiveness beyond website usage data. The extent to which Information Providers use intermediaries (such as libraries and non-profit organizations) to connect with users, for example, is not clear. Only one Information Provider described how the relationships they have built with community organizations enable them to work directly with the individuals to whom those organizations provide services. In that situation, an organization serving Spanish-speaking populations was instrumental for the Information Provider in setting up a focus group to collect data during the development of a Spanish-language mirror site. Inasmuch as this type of dialogue between Information Providers and target users does not appear to be the norm, we must consider the implications of Information Providers engaging in content development, website design, and outreach without input from either individuals within groups that make up the target audience *or* actual users.

And so, Information Providers may see upward trends in site usage but they can only speculate as to the reasons for this growth. Based on the survey and interview data, it is not clear, for example, if Information Providers are "circling back" to intermediaries that assist with outreach to find out what these organizations are in fact doing (e.g., are librarians who have received training on the site showing it to patrons?). Nor is it clear whether the outreach efforts are actually working (e.g., are the patrons then using the site?).

Information Providers know that people are finding them via search engines; however, as evidenced by the following quotes, questions remain about the level of awareness about the sites among their target users:

- "I really have a sense, a hunch that it's not well known—that the site is still not well-known . . . [a]mong any group. I don't think any group you could name knows it as well as we would think. . . . And even though we've been around for ages and there are people who are very supportive in the access to justice commission community . . . [a]nd still you go into clerk's offices and they're like, 'oh, wow, this is new.' And it's not."
- "I don't know if people even think to go on the website for a legal problem."

Because of this lack of knowledge, there is a tendency among Information Providers to make assumptions that what they are doing is working based on the site usage numbers they are seeing.

This lack of knowledge, in turn, makes it more difficult for Information Providers to articulate the impact of statewide legal information websites and thus to gain support within their organization, as well as within the broader legal services community. But now more than ever, it is vitally important for Information Providers to be able to make strong, convincing cases for the value of statewide legal information websites. Since the early years of the websites' development, Information Providers have been encouraged to incorporate evaluation into their regular activities. Several recommendations set forth in the report summarizing findings from the 2004 Statewide Legal Information Website Study (Melton et al., 2005) specifically reference evaluation. For example,

> *Recommendation Seven: A Partnership Strategy*
> Website staff and managers should have a clear partnership building strategy that reaches out to the key actual and potential stakeholders for buy-in, content, marketing, access partnerships, evaluation, and funding.
>
> *Recommendation Fourteen: Evaluation*
> Website staff and managers should have an evaluation strategy that provides the feedback necessary to strengthen the sit [*sic*], and maximizes its service capacity and effectiveness.

The report encouraged website managers and staff to design a strategy that focuses on the "overall comprehensibility and utility of the site" (p. 28). More than ten years later, across the network of statewide legal information websites, the progress is markedly uneven. As noted in the 2007 Circuit Rider program report, website coordinators tend to focus on content development rather than activities that are viewed as more peripheral, such as outreach and evaluation. Moreover, this failure to develop a culture of ongoing evaluative efforts very much reflects a pervasive problem facing the legal services community, namely, "deep-seated obstacles to effective program assessment—'the lack of clear and objective standards' and 'the insufficiency of data concerning the satisfaction of clients, the quality of assistance, and its impact on the individuals and communities served'" (Alfieri, 2013).

To date, the evaluation of many statewide legal information websites has principally involved an ongoing review of website usage statistics. The reliance on these numbers stems largely from the fact that they do not have other data with which to make their case. This is due to the difficulties that Information Providers face in connecting with website users who, for the most part, are anonymous. Even one of the few interviewees who has conducted focus groups in connection with the website noted the difficulty in recruiting participants. Part of this difficulty, she suggested, is due to the life circumstances of many self-represented litigants, leading the Information Provider and her staff to try different approaches:

> I'm always surprised by [the difficulty with recruiting participants] because . . . we recruit people through our legal aid partners and through self-help desks through the courthouse—these are people clearly who are lower income, who, you know, 20 dollars for an hour of their time should be meaningful, right? And, we still have a very difficult time getting people and I think that it's largely [that] the nature of that demographic group is that, you know, when you are sort of living in an uncertain environment . . . it's not easy to plan anything because you never know what's going to happen tomorrow and so I think that's the reality of the people that we're trying to serve and we just need to find a little better way to get them engaged and maybe we could try to do . . . the usability less formally. We can just sort of do it ad hoc—like, today we're going to go over to the court and pull people who are ready and put them in a room and talk to them. Just listen to them really.

Another Information Provider echoed this sentiment about the difficulty of getting users more directly involved—she expressed an interest in including clients of legal services organizations on the site's advisory committee but acknowledged that, for many of them, participation would be difficult (i.e., are they willing and able to miss work to attend an advisory committee meeting?).

Given these difficulties, the reliance on site usage data is understandable. Information Providers, however, specifically mentioned that a key limitation of Google Analytics (the tool most frequently referenced by study participants) is that this data cannot tell them if site users are members of their target audience. This is only the tip of the iceberg, though—other information that cannot be gleaned from site usage data but that Information Providers would like to know includes the following:

Is the information on the site helpful?: "[H]ere's what I would love to know—I would love to know if it's helpful information. You know, the only time I hear from my users is when they're frustrated or when they're not finding what they need or what they think should be there. . . . so I would love to know what's going on with the other people who have come to the site and downloaded the brochure or gotten a form or found a referral to their local legal services program. I would love to know down the stream if [it] was at all useful to them. I assume so. I'd like to think so, but I don't know."

Can they use the information?: "I would like to know if they have the ability to use what we're making or creating for them and if it's really helping them. I would love to know what the outcome is of the situation—you know, if somebody is getting evicted and they find the eviction pamphlet, can they actually . . . advocate for themselves? And what happens at the end? And . . . I'd like to know if . . . when they read the pamphlet, are we really explaining things to them—you know, when you're kind of reading something and all of a sudden you realize that you're understanding it and getting it? You kind of realize, 'Oh, OK, this is making sense.' I kind of wish there was some way I could gauge that."

What else would help them?: "I wish they'd give us more feedback about what would make the website better. . . . I'd love to get more information about what else they need, what else they would want."

How did they use it?: "[I]t would be really helpful to know if there was—if the content that people found is content they used and how did they use it. Did they just use it to inform themselves or understand the law better, what their rights and responsibilities are? Or did they use it to create a document that they sent to another person or to a company to help them accomplish x, y, z? Or did they use it to create a document that they brought to court, and then did it work? You know, was it any good? So that's the kind of information that would be really useful to me because I would want to then try to develop more materials along those lines."

Each of these questions centers around whether the site is meeting the needs of its target users. They are, in effect, asking about the impacts of the resources and services that Information Providers are providing through statewide legal information websites. The overarching question then becomes, How do you measure impact in this environment? One interviewee, in talking about evaluation activities, suggested that measuring outcomes was impossible with statewide legal information websites because the population served is comprised of anonymous website users.

Perhaps it is not a matter of taking on the impossible but rather requires a fundamental shift in the way in which we approach the evaluation of statewide legal information websites and related initiatives. The importance of website usage data is not being contested; however, as observed by several Information Providers, those numbers fail to tell the whole story. In the interest of filling the existing gaps in information that preclude Information Providers from knowing how they are doing, we must introduce a paradigm shift. This shift entails viewing the websites as programs and then designing and implementing evaluation activities accordingly. Underlying this approach is the perspective that these websites are an extension of traditional legal services rather than technology projects that exist somewhat separately from these traditional services. The recommended approach is also grounded in an understanding that the so-called human issues related to development and maintaining these websites (e.g., partnership building, identifying user needs) are central to these efforts.

MAKING THE CASE FOR PROGRAM EVALUATION

In making this paradigm shift, the first hurdle to overcome is defining statewide legal information websites as programs—they exist in a somewhat gray space, as many individuals within the legal services community still struggle to understand why they exist and how they fit into the broader access to justice framework. Royse, Thyer, and Padgett (2009), however, define a program as "an organized collection of activities designed to reach certain objectives" (p. 5). Statewide legal information websites—many of which have a statement of purpose or mission listed on the site that is related to the provision of legal information and services to their target users—fit within this definition. The extent to which they have an identity distinct from the organization that maintains them varies from state to state, due to differences in funding and staffing. Almost every website has a distinct presence (even if it is part of the organization's general website) and presumably has an impact that can be measured apart from the organization's other activities.

Their current situation will influence the type of evaluation that Information Providers feel prepared to undertake at this time. Common evaluation strategies include needs assessment, formative evaluation, process evaluation, and outcome evaluation (Patton, 1987; Rossi & Freeman, 1989; Royse et al., 2009). A formative evaluation, for example, may be beneficial to Information Providers working on recently launched or redesigned websites who are interested in gathering information to improve their current operations. Given the legal services community's focus on demonstrating effectiveness, however, outcome measurement may be the most important type of evaluation activity for many Information Providers.

In recent years, practitioners and scholars within the non-profit sector have become increasingly focused on the measurement of outcomes (Herman & Renz, 2008; Morino, 2011; Penna, 2011), and Information Providers can benefit from the rich literature in this area. The results of the program (i.e., what has changed) are the outcomes (Ridge, 2010). Morino (2011), using key concepts from leading works in the area of outcomes assessment, defines outcomes as "[s]ocially meaningful changes for those served by a program, generally defined in terms of expected changes in knowledge, skills, attitudes, behavior, condition, or status" (p. 11). Outcomes are closely related to effectiveness, defined by Berk and Rossi (1990) as "the extent to which a policy or program is achieving its goals and purposes" (p. 15).

The first—and arguably most important—task is selecting an appropriate outcome to measure. The current evaluation activities of Information Providers focus on outputs rather than outcomes. Website usage data is an output, comparable to client counts and attendance in evaluations of traditional social services programs (Saxton, Naumer, & Fisher, 2007). As observed by Patton (1987),

> [i]t makes sense to count . . . the number [of people] who receive or report some concrete benefit from the program. There are many attributes of programs, however, that do not lend themselves to counting. Even the scaling of quality attributes is an inadequate way of capturing either program quality or the effect of a program on the quality of life experienced by participants following the program. (p. 29)

What, then, are the effects upon which Information Providers should focus? There is growing recognition within the legal services community that effectiveness cannot be narrowly defined in terms of legal outcomes (i.e., whether someone prevails in court) (Albiston & Sandefur, 2013). This is certainly true within the context of statewide legal information websites. A statewide legal information website user, for example, may not prevail in court because the respondent raises a valid affirmative defense. In this scenario, the legal outcome has nothing to do with whether the site effectively provided the user with information applicable to his situation or with guidance on how to bring the matter into the legal system.

Information Providers are likely to think of outcomes in different terms, given the various approaches they have adopted in developing and maintaining their statewide legal information websites. Currently, the websites exist along a continuum, with some focusing primarily on providing information resources and others using the website as a vehicle to provide legal services to eligible individuals. The latter approach is reflected in the growing number of initiatives that seek to integrate the website with online intake and triage services. Underlying these different approaches are different ideas about the purpose of the site: Is it to provide basic information? Is it to facilitate transactions with the court (e.g., through online forms)? Or is it to transform the relationship between individuals with legal needs and legal services providers?[1]

Notwithstanding these differences, all Information Providers need to think about the specific user needs that the site aims to address. Saxton et al. (2007) developed a logic model in connection with assessing the effectiveness of 2-1-1 services. This model set forth a range of outcomes (short term, mid-term, and long term) for individuals, organizations, and society. By way of example, short-term and mid-term outcomes for individuals include immediate answers and comprehensive solving of problems, respectively. In a similar vein, one possible outcome associated with statewide legal information websites is that a user is able to locate information on the website that answers the question that brought him to the website and he is able to understand how that information applies to his particular situation.

Other Information Providers may be more concerned with outcomes related to online document assembly—for example, was the user's form accepted for filing by the court? Regardless of the specific outcome identified, however, effectiveness should be measured from the point of view of users, as well as of Information Providers and other stakeholders (e.g., external funders). Different stakeholders are likely to have somewhat divergent interests. Information Providers, for instance, are operating within resource constraints about which users may be unaware. As such, it is prudent to identify outcome measures for different stakeholders (as done by Saxton et al. [2007]).

For many Information Providers, identifying the outcome to measure may be less problematic than figuring out *how* to measure it. That Information Providers are trying to gather information from typically anonymous website users, rather than clients who are walking through the door, is a significant challenge. To answer questions about whether target users are able to use resources and services available through a statewide legal information website effectively, Information Providers must bridge the gap that currently exists between themselves and their users. The study detailed in chapters 4 and 5 revealed how collaboration underlies most Information Providers' efforts in the areas of content development and outreach. In contrast, it appears that only a few states have implemented evaluation efforts that leverage the resources and connections of the organizations with which they typically collaborate. The efforts undertaken to date, however, aptly demonstrate how other access to justice stakeholder organizations can expand their intermediary role in meaningful ways—they can move beyond increasing awareness about the website to connecting Information Providers with actual users and/or individuals with unmet legal needs who could benefit from using the site.

In many cases, users may have direct interactions with any number of the access to justice stakeholder organizations with which Information Providers collaborate. Building on this premise, below is a brief outline of user-centered program evaluation activities that require Information Providers to leverage existing collaborative relationships to connect with users. It has elements of both "community-based participatory research" (CBPR) and "participatory action research" (PAR). As described by Charn and Selbin (2013), "CBPR has emerged as a new paradigm to make research more inclusive and relevant by bringing together academics and communities to address community priorities. PAR strives to produce knowledge and change at the same time. Challenges abound, but so do opportunities. The potential . . . to help answer pressing questions about community needs, delivery models, and service efficacy has never been greater." (p. 169).

Many of the Information Providers interviewed indicated that their current limited evaluation activities were due not to a lack of interest, but rather to a belief that they lacked the resources to do more at this time. Like content development and outreach, though, evaluation can be a collaborative effort, as described below. Moreover, Information Providers do not have to reinvent the wheel when planning evaluation activities—both LSC and Pro Bono Net have made tools and resources available to Information Providers, and states can look to what others have done in terms of evaluation activities. Both organizations, for example, make project evaluation reports available that can serve as guidance for Information Providers trying to identify appropriate evaluation methods and data collection strategies. LSNTAP also provides general guidance on evaluating technology projects, as well as reports of specific initiatives (e.g., the online survey tool used in Georgia deployed to obtain feedback from a dispersed population).

The proposed framework for user-centered program evaluation draws from current practices identified by Information Providers, as well as from research done in the area of user-centered e-government (Bertot & Jaeger, 2006; de Róiste, 2013; Pietersen et al., 2007) and information services (Fisher, Durrance, & Hinton, 2004; Saxton et al., 2007; Sim & Rocha, 1998). These evaluation activities can provide more substantial evidence of value than the Google Analytics upon which many Information Providers rely; it can lay the groundwork for the next iteration of statewide legal information websites that are designed with the "user's world view" at the center of the process (Westbrook, 2008, p. 35). This framework is not intended to be a detailed prescription for Information Providers to follow but rather to offer general guidance on how they can engage in evaluation efforts that will provide them with information about the effectiveness of their current efforts. As illustrated in figure 7.1, it calls for Information Providers to assess the current legal information needs of their users, the readability and understandability of current site content, the usability of the site overall, and the quality of documents created with the assistance of services available through the site. And, while this discussion focuses on statewide

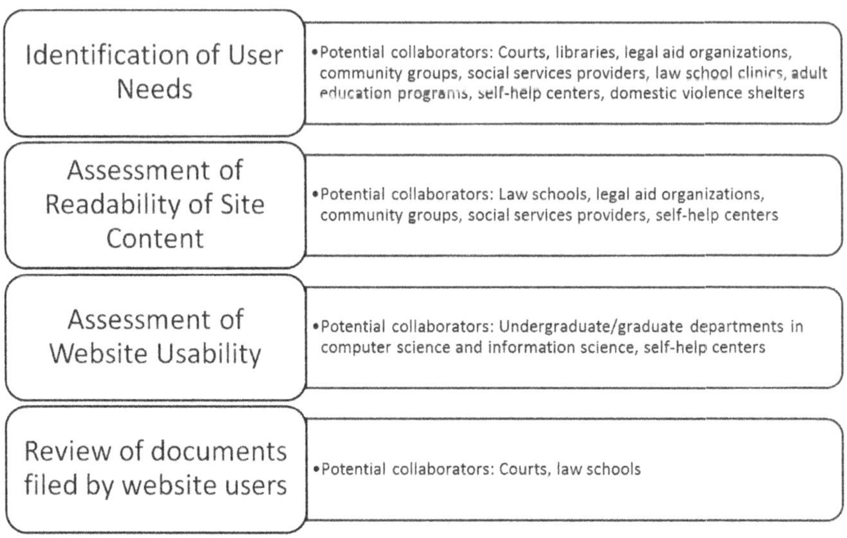

Figure 7.1. Proposed Framework for User-Centered Program Evaluation

legal information websites, the proposed framework can be easily modified for use with respect to other technology-enabled access to justice initiatives.

IDENTIFICATION OF CURRENT USER NEEDS

Several Information Providers indicated that findings from legal needs studies were used to identify areas of focus during the initial phase of content development. As noted by Sandefur and Smyth (2011), though, "in most states, the public's civil legal needs are not routinely assessed and no entity can ensure that services in specific areas match the needs of the eligible populations in those areas" (p. v). Moreover, these general legal needs studies, even if current, may not tell Information Providers everything they need to know. For example, a legal needs study conducted in Kansas in 2011 addressed issues such as whether individuals have Internet access, as well as their interest in accessing legal information online. However, it did not address potential barriers to intellectual access (i.e., whether individuals could understand and apply the legal information they read online).

The needs assessment recommended here has a somewhat narrower focus than the legal needs studies conducted to date. While needs assessments are typically seen as a preliminary evaluation activity (Royse et al., 2009), needs evolve over time and Information Providers may want to verify that the initial needs identified are still prevalent today. The data collected through a needs "reassessment" would guide the other evaluation efforts—what are the legal issues that lead users to the website? What types of resources are they looking for? What are the difficulties they face in accessing information on the site (in terms of both physical and intellectual barriers)? The collection of this information would involve reaching out directly to the various stakeholders with whom Information Providers collaborate—for example, courts, libraries, legal aid and other non-profit organizations, and social services agencies. Information Providers can turn to tools developed by the LSC (as part of its Client Website Evaluation System) to assist with conducting this type of community needs assessment.[2] The Community Provider Survey, for example, can be used to gather "information from other legal services providers, social services providers and community groups about the visibility and usefulness of the website." Questions include the following: (1) For what type of legal issues do you refer those whom you assist to the website? and (2) What do users typically have trouble with or ask for help with when using the website?

These community stakeholders, in addition to providing their perspectives on user needs, can serve as a direct link to users. LSNTAP, in training materials posted on its website, suggests that students in community education courses, law school clinic clients, and HUD Neighborhood Network users can play an important role in evaluation (LSNTAP, n.d.). Whether or not an Information Provider has access to any of these groups depends largely on their existing relationships, however. The above-referenced focus group convened by one Information Provider in connection with her state's recently developed Spanish-language site is an example of this approach. Although the proposed evaluation framework emphasizes the importance of connecting with actual users, gaining input from individuals who belong to target user groups is valuable at this early stage.

There are ways, however, that actual users may be reachable at this stage. Information Providers in several states have conducted outreach at domestic violence shelters and public libraries; others work closely with self-help centers throughout their state. The Community Provider Survey would provide information about whether partner organizations are in fact telling their clients and patrons about the site. If that is the case, Information Providers could then work with staff members at these partner organizations to talk with a group of clients (or patrons) about their information needs and their experiences with using the statewide legal information website.

This type of needs assessment is a significant step above the anecdotal evidence upon which many Information Providers currently rely, even if does not involve collecting data from random samples of either community stakeholders or website users. As noted in the instructions for the Community Provider Survey, "even if the data produced from such samples cannot meet the requisite criteria for scientific reliability, they nonetheless can provide program managers with valuable practical knowledge with which to assess system design and operations and make appropriate adjustments."

ASSESSMENT OF READABILITY OF EXISTING CONTENT

Once the Information Providers have a clearer picture of their users' information needs and the barriers they face in accessing information based upon the community needs assessment outlined above, they can turn their focus to evaluating the extent to which the website currently meets those needs. This involves examining content available on the site to determine if it is readable and understandable by users.

This part of the evaluation can be comprised of two strategies. The first is a systematic review of a selection of content in the legal content areas identified as most important during the community needs assessment using one of the available tools for analyzing reading grade level, such as (1) the Flesch-Kincaid Grade Level Score (in Word or WordPerfect), as was done in the recent study by Dyson and Schellenberg (2016) or (2) OpenAdvocate WriteClearly (a free web-based tool). In addition, using plain-language resources available online (e.g., the Maryland Access to Justice Commission's "Writing for Self-Represented Litigants" [2012] or Legal Assistance of Western New York Inc.'s "The Essential Plain Language Collection" [n.d]), Information Providers can create a checklist of plain-language best practices and review the selected content items against this checklist.

In conducting this part of the evaluation, Information Providers may want to leverage existing relationships with law schools. As discussed in chapter 6, one Information Provider is currently providing clear writing training to law students enrolled in a brief advice clinic as well as working with them on writing content for the statewide legal information website. This approach has been praised by Staudt (2013), who has been advocating for law schools to develop clinic-based opportunities through which students can "learn core competencies needed in an increasingly technological profession, while they build tools and write content to help low-income, self-represented litigants overcome serious barriers in their pursuit of justice" (Staudt, 2013). Similarly, Charn and Selbin (2013) and Alfieri (2013) call for an expanded role for law school clinics in empirical research. Several of the reasons they cite—their ties to client communities and their access to expertise and data—highlight why clinics could play a role in program evaluation. Involving law students in plain-language review is just one way that they could contribute to evaluation efforts while also providing them with marketable skills that will make them more effective practitioners when they enter the workforce.

These readability assessments could be supplemented with focus groups that ideally, once again, would be comprised of website users with whom Information Providers can connect through their partners. During focus group sessions, users can be asked to review a small number of articles, brochures, or other written materials and then, as a group, asked questions aimed at assessing whether they comprehended what they just read. For example, after having participants read an article about obtaining a garnishment, questions can be asked about whether they understand what a garnishment is and what information is needed to complete a request and writ for garnishment.

ASSESSMENT OF WEBSITE USABILITY

Bertot and Jaeger (2008) cite usability testing as a key methodology to be employed in user-centered e-government evaluations.[3] Usability testing is not a novel concept with statewide legal information websites—Pro Bono Net conducted it before rolling out the latest iteration of the LawHelp platform, and a couple of Information Providers discussed their experiences with this form of evaluation. The majority of Information Providers who participated in this study, however, have not conducted usability testing.

Usability testing is related to the readability assessments described above and, in fact, can be viewed as the other piece of the puzzle of figuring out whether users have intellectual access to site content. As observed by Bertot and Jaeger (2006), usability testing can explore whether "navigation and orientation are intuitive; elements of the site perform as users anticipate; elements of the site are clearly labeled; [and] instructions are meaningful and easy to follow" (p. 165). Thus, while the readability assessments focus on specific items of content, usability testing can look across the site to evaluate if users can address the information need that brought them to the site. This is particularly important as statewide legal information websites become increasingly interactive, with the addition of online forms and intake systems. For example, usability testing can provide valuable information about whether a step-by-step process for completing a form is intuitive or likely to leave a user frustrated due to a failure to define key legal terms or provide detailed instructions. Usability testing, as noted by Westbrook (2009), can help identify what helps people move through a problem-solving process.

One option for Information Providers to consider is approaching undergraduate or graduate classes in computer science or information science departments about making usability testing a project for one of their classes. This approach was employed in both states where usability testing has been conducted and is similar to the translation projects developed by another Information Provider. Those Information Providers with usability testing experience, however, acknowledged the difficulties they have had in recruiting participants. To overcome these challenges, one suggested a more informal approach. If the problem is getting participants to commit in advance to coming to a usability testing at a designated time, one possible solution is to move the usability testing into a self-help center operated out of a library or courthouse. Participants would not have to make an advance commitment but rather would only have to spend extra time at the self-help center that day (i.e., after they have addressed the purpose of their visit). Moreover, conducting the usability test at a self-help center may make it a less intimidating experience for users, as they will already have some familiarity with the environment, thus removing another potential barrier to participation.

REVIEW OF DOCUMENTS FILED BY WEBSITE USERS

The fourth component of the proposed evaluation framework requires collaboration with a different access to justice stakeholder—the courts. Several study participants mentioned past and present collaborative efforts with courts to track documents filed by users as they make their way through the court system. Here, the purpose of tracking documents is not to determine the legal outcome but rather to see if the user is able to navigate their way through the system to the point at which a judgment is rendered. The user's success, for example, in completing a divorce petition through an automated document preparation system built into the statewide legal information website is evidence that he was provided with sufficient information to navigate that particular process. If the website leads users through the process of electronically filing documents, a successful filing is further evidence of the helpfulness of the instructions and guidance offered through the website.

There are several limitations to this particular evaluation effort—it can only be employed with those statewide legal information websites that provide some type of access to online forms. Moreover, the ability to track the forms is dependent upon users only being able to create them through the automated document preparation system or the court making some type of designation when it accepts a document for filing. As a practical matter, even if Information Providers could recruit law students to assist with this venture, it is a labor-intensive endeavor that could only be undertaken in connection with a limited set of case filings. When combined with the other evaluation efforts described above, however, a pilot evaluation study of this nature could provide valuable information about what users are able to accomplish through the website.

A CALL FOR FUTURE RESEARCH . . . AND A CALL FOR FUTURE ACTION

The proposed framework for user-centered program evaluation described above can be used to assess the effectiveness of the approach adopted by any given state. For those involved in technology-enabled access to justice projects, the proposed evaluation activities, together with findings from the current study about the role of collaboration in overcoming challenges related to funding and staffing, can help them fill in any gaps they might have in terms of user needs and preferences. Each user-centered program evaluation can also provide a road map for other states that may be interested in adopting a similar approach.

Individual program evaluations can also lay the groundwork for a comprehensive research agenda that will benefit the entire access to justice community. Looking beyond statewide legal information websites, future research should include in-depth explorations of how various community stakeholders (e.g., courts, libraries) are working together to connect self-help users with the legal information they need. Libraries are increasingly seen as a natural partner in access to justice initiatives, but little is known about what these partnerships look like in practice. Such research would be a valuable contribution to the growing body of research in the area of community-based partnerships that seek to provide enhanced services through innovative uses of technology (Jaeger et al., 2015; Taylor et al., 2014). Empirical studies that shed light on how libraries work with legal services organizations and courts (which may have quite different goals and priorities) would be an important step toward building a model of legal services–library collaboration that could be replicated in a variety of contexts. A multi-site case study of self-help centers housed in public law libraries, for example, could explore many of the literacy issues discussed throughout this book.

In the introduction, it was observed that the legal services community has been criticized for its lack of empirical research upon which to make decisions about resource allocation. A commitment to evaluation research focused on outcomes and impacts is one answer to this criticism, and the user-centered evaluation framework outlined above is one avenue for future research. Opportunities abound for research that bridges theory and practice, and it is only by building these bridges that we can fully examine the delivery of legal services in this country. Community-based research that brings together the perspectives of a diverse group of access to justice stakeholders—from the administrators of the highest courts to self-represented litigants—is, now more than ever, vital.

The research is not an end in itself, however. It is a foundation upon which future policy and practice in the arena of legal services can be built. The importance of these efforts cannot be overstated, as the seemingly intractable justice gap is one of the most pervasive social problems of our time. Almost a century ago, Reginald Heber Smith, in *Justice and the Poor* (1919), observed that ongoing developments in legal service are

> of direct concern not only to the fair administration of justice, but to the well-being of the nation. It is of high importance that such developments be encouraged and supported, not for the sake of the legal aid organizations themselves, . . . but because in them, with all their faults and weaknesses, is contained our best immediate hope for a realization of our ideal of such an equal administration of the laws that denial of justice on account of poverty shall forever be made impossible in America. (p. 249)

This remains true today, and a commitment to research that can shape and improve the delivery of legal services in the United States may be our "best immediate hope" for making definitive progress toward closing the justice gap.

NOTES

1. This concept of transformation is borrowed from the e-government literature: "[T]ransformation means that e-government will cause or permit the relationship between citizens and governments to fundamentally change in positive ways, generally producing much more citizen-centric and responsive government" (Coursey & Norris, 2008, p. 524). See also Baum & Di Maio (2000).

2. Although LSC only requires recipients of new and renewal website grants to complete these evaluations, they provide a useful framework for all Information Providers as they think about implementing more rigorous evaluations.

3. Accessibility testing, another important methodology noted by Bertot and Jaeger (2008), can involve both user testing and expert testing. To the extent that Information Providers may find it difficult to connect with users who have disabilities (even with the assistance of collaborators), accessibility testing is not part of the user-centered evaluation set forth here. It is worth noting, however, that Information Providers' very limited discussion of accessibility in response to survey and interview questions raises interesting questions about their awareness of the particular needs of individuals with disabilities that are worth exploring in a future study.

Appendix A

List of Statewide Legal Information Websites

Alabama	http://www.alabamalegalhelp.org
Alaska	http://alaskalawhelp.org
Arizona	http://www.azlawhelp.org
Arkansas	http://www.arlegalservices.org
California	http://lawhelpca.org
Colorado	http://lawhelp.coloradolegalservices.org
Connecticut	http://ctlawhelp.org
Delaware	http://www.lscd.com
District of Columbia	http://www.lawhelp.org/DC
Florida	http://floridalawhelp.org
Georgia	http://www.georgialegalaid.org
Hawaii	http://www.lawhelp.org/hi
Idaho	http://www.idaholegalaid.org
Illinois	https://www.illinoislegalaid.org
Indiana	http://www.indianalegalservices.org
Iowa	http://www.iowalegalaid.org
Kansas	http://www.kansaslegalservices.org
Kentucky	http://kyjustice.org
Louisiana	http://louisianalawhelp.org
Maine	http://ptla.org
Maryland	https://www.peoples-law.org
Massachusetts	http://www.masslegalhelp.org
Michigan	http://michiganlegalhelp.org
Minnesota	http://www.lawhelpmn.org
Mississippi	http://www.mslegalservices.org

Missouri	http://www.lsmo.org
Montana	http://www.montanalawhelp.org
Nebraska	http://www.legalaidofnebraska.org
Nevada	http://nevadalawhelp.org
New Hampshire	http://www.nhls.org
New Jersey	http://www.lsnjlaw.org
New Mexico	http://lawhelpnewmexico.org
New York	http://www.lawhelpny.org
North Carolina	http://www.lawhelpnc.org
North Dakota	http://www.legalassist.org
Ohio	http://www.ohiolegalservices.org/public/legal_problem
Oklahoma	http://oklaw.org
Oregon	http://oregonlawhelp.org
Pennsylvania	http://www.palawhelp.org
Rhode Island	http://www.helprilaw.org
South Carolina	http://www.lawhelp.org/sc
South Dakota	http://helpsouthdakota.com
Tennessee	http://www.help4tn.org
Texas	http://texaslawhelp.org
Utah	http://www.utahlegalservices.org
Vermont	http://www.vtlawhelp.org
Virginia	http://www.valegalaid.org
Washington	http://www.washingtonlawhelp.org
West Virginia	http://www.lawv.net
Wisconsin	http://www.badgerlaw.net
Wyoming	http://www.lawyoming.org

Appendix B

Survey Questions

Are you currently involved with maintaining a statewide legal information website?

1. If yes, please indicate which statewide legal website you work on:
2. If yes, please briefly describe your current role in connection with the statewide legal information website:
3. If no, were you previously involved in maintaining a statewide legal information website?
   - If yes, please indicate which statewide legal information website you worked on:
   - If yes, please briefly describe your current role in connection with the statewide legal information website:

INITIAL WEBSITE DEVELOPMENT

1. How long ago was the website launched?
   ___Within the past 12 months
   ___1–3 years ago
   ___4–6 years ago
   ___7–10 years ago
   ___More than 10 years ago
   ___I'm not sure
2. Please provide the names of the organizations initially involved in the development of the website:

3. For whom was the website developed?

General public	___Yes	___No	___Don't know
Low-income individuals	___Yes	___No	___Don't know
Self-represented (pro se) litigants	___Yes	___No	___Don't know
Legal services providers	___Yes	___No	___Don't know
Information intermediaries (e.g., librarians, social service providers)	___Yes	___No	___Don't know

Other (please specify):

4. What were the perceived legal consumer information and/or support needs that you sought to address through this website?
5. How were the major legal needs of target users initially identified?
6. Please describe any unexpected obstacles that were encountered during the initial development of the website:

CURRENT WEBSITE PRACTICES

7. What organizations are currently involved in maintaining the site?
8. Do you create content for the site? For the purposes of this survey, "content" refers to legal information provided to the site's target users.
   - If yes, is anyone else involved in content creation?
   - If yes, what other individuals are involved in content creation (e.g., volunteer attorneys, Legal Aid staff)?
   - If no, who creates content for the site?
9. How many significant revisions has the site undergone since its initial development? "Significant revisions" include changes to the overall design of the site as well as to content on the site.
   ___None
   ___1
   ___2
   ___More than 3
   If yes, can you briefly describe the nature of these revisions?
10. How often is content reviewed?
   ___Never
   ___Irregularly
   ___At least once a month
   ___At least once every six months
   ___At least once a year

11. Is there a process in place for identifying needed changes and updates to the website?
    ___Yes
    ___No
    If yes, please describe:
12. How is information about the website disseminated?

Print media	___Yes	___No
Legal service providers	___Yes	___No
Social service agencies	___Yes	___No
Courts	___Yes	___No
Libraries	___Yes	___No
Listservs	___Yes	___No
Social media	___Yes	___No

    Other (please specify):
13. Does the organization seek the input of any of the following types of stakeholders?

Elected officials	___Yes	___No
Social service agencies	___Yes	___No
Courts	___Yes	___No
Libraries	___Yes	___No
Local non-profit/community organizations	___Yes	___No
Minority group leadership	___Yes	___No

    Other (please specify):
14. Does the organization have regular working relationships with the following entities?

Other legal services projects/programs within the state	___Yes	___No
Law schools within the state	___Yes	___No
State and local bar associations	___Yes	___No

15. A) What are the main challenges you face related to the development of website content?
    B) What measures have you taken to address these challenges?
16. A) What are the main challenges you face related to the design of the website?
    B) What measures have you taken to address these challenges?

BARRIERS TO INFORMATION ACCESS FOR WEBSITE USERS

17. What, if any, barriers do you think your users face in accessing information on the site (check all that apply)?

Limited literacy	___Yes	___No
Lack of understanding of legal terminology	___Yes	___No
Limited English-language proficiency	___Yes	___No
Lack of Internet access	___Yes	___No
Lack of digital literacy skills	___Yes	___No
Disabilities (e.g., visual/hearing impairments)	___Yes	___No

Other (please specify):

18. Please briefly describe actions undertaken to overcome the barriers identified in question 16.
19. Is the site compatible with mobile devices?
    If no, do you think this poses a barrier to users? Why or why not?

WEBSITE USAGE

20. Who do you think uses your website on a regular basis?

General public	___Yes	___No
Low-income individuals	___Yes	___No
Self-represented (pro se) litigants	___Yes	___No
Legal services providers	___Yes	___No
Information intermediaries (e.g., librarians, social services providers)	___Yes	___No

Other (please specify):

21. Do you collect website usage data?
    If yes, how often do you analyze this data?
    ___Never
    ___Irregularly
    ___At least once a month
    ___At least once every six months
    ___At least once a year
    If yes, can you provide the following information?

Total number of visitors in 2012:
Total number of visitors in 2013:
Total page views in 2012:
Total page views in 2013:
Most frequently visited pages in 2012:
Most frequently visited pages in 2013:
If yes, please provide a brief summary of what you learned from this data the last time you analyzed it:

22. Do you collect demographic information from users (e.g., income, family size, location of residence)?

Location of residence	___Yes	___No
Family size	___Yes	___No
Income	___Yes	___No
Race/ethnicity	___Yes	___No

If yes, can you specify the types of demographic information you collect?
Other (please specify):

23. Do you solicit feedback from users?

Through an online feedback form	___Yes	___No
Through e-mail	___Yes	___No
Through personal discussion	___Yes	___No

If yes, how is it obtained?
Other (please specify):
If yes, what are some of the most common requests you receive from users?
If yes, what are some of the most common compliments you receive from users?
If yes, what are some of the most common complaints you receive from users?

24. To what extent do you think the website currently meets your users' information needs?

1	2	3	4	5
Not at all	To a Limited Extent	Somewhat	Mostly	Completely

Please explain:

25. In your opinion, what types of information should be added to your website to increase user satisfaction?

Appendix C

State Profiles

State Designation	*Geographic Region*	*Total Population*[1]	*% Below Poverty*[2] *National Average: 15.8%*	*Access to Justice Commission?*	*# of Attorneys/ 10,000 People in Poverty*[3]	*Total Funding for LSC-funded Programs*[4]	*% of Population Lacking Basic Prose Literacy Skills*[5]	*% of Population Who Have Earned a High School Diploma (or More)*[6] *National Average: 85.3%*
S1	West	730,307	9.3	Yes	2.44	$3,617,695	9	91.4
S2	South	4,817,528	18.7	Yes	0.62	$7,625,744	15	82.1
S3	South	2,949,828	19.7	Yes	0.8	$7,777,724	14	82.4
S4	West	37,999,878	16.8	Yes	0.96	$104,590,206	23	80.6
S5	West	5,189,458	13.0	Yes	0.56	$9,027,498	10	89.3
S6	Northeast	3,591,765	10.7	No	1.85	$2,590,536	9	88.6
S7	South	633,427	18.9	Yes	8.82	$1,555,740	19	87.1
S8	South	19,320,749	17.0	Yes	0.87	$42,046,431	20	85.3
S9	South	9,915,646	19.0	Equal Justice Commission	0.56	$20,794,498	17	83.9
S10	Midwest	3,075,039	12.7	No	1.19	$7,872,974	7	90.5
S11	Midwest	1,595,590	15.6	No	0.71	$2,387,025	11	88.4
S12	Midwest	12,868,192	14.7	Equal Justice Foundation	1.02	$34,440,088	13	86.4
S13	Midwest	6,537,782	15.9	Pro Bono Commission	0.92	$8,449,493	8	86.6
S14	Midwest	2,885,398	14.0	No	0.69	$5,470,072	8	89.7
S15	South	4,602,134	19.8	No	1.37	$12,988,067	16	82.2
S16	Northeast	6,645,303	11.9	Yes	2.38	$9,167,694	10	89.0
S17	Northeast	1,328,501	14.0	Yes	1.72	$6,374,451	7	90.2
S18	Midwest	9,882,519	17.0	No	0.69	$23,532,054	8	87.9

S19	Midwest	5,379,646	11.2	Yes	1.8	$15,920,405	6	91.5
S20	South	5,884,868	10.1	Yes	3.06	$27,608,013	11	88.2
S21	West	1,005,494	16.5	Yes	0.72	$3,067,152	9	90.8
S22	West	2,083,540	21.9	Yes	0.89	$6,364,700	16	82.8
S23	Midwest	11,553,031	16.0	No	0.91	$39,612,617	9	87.6
S24	South	6,454,914	17.8	Yes	0.56	$17,378,997	13	83.1
S25	South	26,060,796	17.5	Yes	0.43	$59,746,943	19	79.9
S26	Northeast	625,953	12.8	No	2.07	$620,544	7	91.0
S27	West	6,895,318	14.1	Access to Justice Board	1.36	$25,724,888	10	89.7
S28	South	1,856,680	18.5	Yes	1.19	$8,045,657	13	82.8

[1] U.S. Census Bureau, 2013 Population Estimates, retrieved from http://www.census.gov/popest/data/index.html.

[2] U.S. Census Bureau (2014), Poverty: 2012 and 2013, American Community Survey Briefs, retrieved from http://www.census.gov/content/dam/Census/library/publications/2014/acs/acsbr13-01.pdf.

[3] National Center for Access to Justice (n.d.), The Justice Index, retrieved from http://www.justiceindex.org/findings/attorney-access.

[4] Legal Services Corporation (2014), LSC by the Numbers 2013: The Data Underlying Legal Aid Programs, retrieved from http://www.lsc.gov/about/lsc-numbers-2013.

[5] National Center for Education Statistics (2003), Indirect Estimate of Percent Lacking Basic Prose Literacy Skills and Corresponding Credible Intervals: All States, retrieved from http://nces.ed.gov/naal/estimates/overview.aspx#4.

[6] U.S. Census Bureau (2012, February), Educational Attainment in the United States: 2009, Current Population Reports, retrieved from https://www.census.gov/prod/2012pubs/p20-566.pdf.

Bibliography

Aaron, K. (2012, Dec. 7). "Don't forget your court date": How text messages and other technology can give legal support to the poor. Retrieved from http://www.slate.com/articles/technology/future_tense/2012/12/legal_aid_text_messaging_automated_call_backs_and_other_tech_enhanced_support.html.

Abel, L. K. (2009). Evidence-based access to justice. *University of Pennsylvania Journal of Law & Social Change, 13*(3), 295–313.

Abel, L. K. (2012). *Turner v. Rogers* and the right of meaningful access to the courts. *Denver University Law Review, 89*, 805–823.

Acosta, L. M., & Cherry, A. M. (2008). Reference services in courts and governmental settings. *Legal Reference Services Quarterly, 26*(1–2), 113–134.

Adeyemon, E. (2009). Integrating digital literacies into outreach services for underserved youth populations. *Reference Librarian, 50*, 85–98.

Agada, John. (1999). Inner-city gatekeepers: An exploratory survey of their information use environment. *Journal of the American Society for Information Science, 50*, 74–85.

Albiston, C. R., & Sandefur, R. L. (2013). Expanding the empirical study of access to justice. *Wisconsin Law Review, 2013*, 101.

Albrecht, R. A., Greacen, J. M., Hough, B. R., & Zorza, R. (2003). Judicial techniques for cases involving self-represented litigants. *The Judges Journal, 42*, 16–48.

Alfieri, A. V. (2013). Community education and access to justice in a time of scarcity: Notes from the West Grove Trolley Garage case. *Wisconsin Law Review, 2013*, 121–143.

American Association of Law Libraries. (2014, July). *Law libraries and access to justice: A report of the American Association of Law Libraries Special Committee on Access to Justice.* Retrieved from http://www.aallnet.org/mm/Publications/products/atjwhitepaper.pdf.

American Bar Association (n.d.). Commission on Interest on Lawyers' Trust Accounts: Overview. Retrieved from http://www.americanbar.org/groups/interest_lawyers_trust_accounts/overview.html.

American Bar Association. (2003). *Handbook on limited scope legal assistance.*

American Bar Association. (2012). *Standards for language access in courts.*

American Bar Association. (2014, Aug.). *An analysis of rules that enable lawyers to serve self-represented litigants.*

American Bar Association. (2016). *Report on the future of legal services in the United States.* Retrieved from http://www.americanbar.org/content/dam/aba/images/abanews/2016FLSReport_FNL_WEB.pdf.

Babbie, E. (2013). *The basics of social research* (6th ed.). Belmont, CA: Cengage Learning.

Barclay, S. (1996). The decision to self-represent. *Social Science Quarterly, 77*(4), 912–923.

Baum, C. H., & Di Maio, A. (2000). *Gartner's four phases of e-government model.* Retrieved from https://www.gartner.com/doc/317292/gartners-phases-egovernment-model.

Berenson, S. K. (2001). A family law residency program? A modest proposal in response to the burdens created by self-represented litigants in family court. *Rutgers Law Journal, 33*(1), 105.

Berk, R. A., & Rossi, P. H. (1990). *Thinking about program evaluation.* Newbury Park, CA: Sage Publications.

Berkman Center for Internet & Society. (2010, July 30). *Best Practices in the Use of Technology to Facilitate Access to Justice Initiatives.* Retrieved from http://cyber.law.harvard.edu/sites/cyber.law.harvard.edu/files/A2J_Report_Final_073010.pdf.

Bertot, J. C. (2003). The multiple dimensions of the digital divide: More than the technology "haves" and "have nots." *Government Information Quarterly, 20*(2), 185–191.

Bertot, J., & Jaeger, P. (2006). User-centered e-government: Challenges and benefits for government web sites. *Government Information Quarterly, 23,* 163–168.

Bertot, J. C., & Jaeger, P. T. (2008). The e-government paradox: Better customer service doesn't necessarily cost less. *Government Information Quarterly, 25,* 149–154.

Bertot, J. C., Real, B., Lee, J., McDermott, A., & Jaeger, P. T. (2015). *2014 Digital Inclusion Survey: Survey findings and results.* Information Policy & Access Center: College Park, Maryland.

Birnbaum, R., & Bala, N. (2012). Views of Ontario lawyers on family litigants without representation. *University of New Brunswick Law Journal, 65,* 99–124.

Bishop, A. P., Tidline, T. J., Shoemaker, S., & Salela, P. (1999). Public libraries and networked information services in low-income communities. *Library & Information Science Research, 21*(3), 361–390.

Blasi, G. (2004). Deborah L. Rhode's access to justice: How much access? How much justice? *Fordham Law Review, 73,* 865–881.

Brodoff, L. (2008). Lifting burdens, proof, social justice, and public assistance administrative hearings. *New York University Review of Law & Social Change, 32,* 131–189.

Brodoff, L., McClellan, S., & Anderson, E. (2003). The ADA: One avenue to appointed counsel before a full civil Gideon. *Seattle Journal for Social Justice, 2*(2), 609–640.

Bruce, T. R. (2000). Public legal information: Focus and future. *University of Sydney Technology Law Review, 2,* 16–35.

Buhai, S. L. (2009). Access to justice for unrepresented litigants: A comparative perspective. *Loyola of Los Angeles Law Review, 42,* 979–1020.

Burnett, G., Jaeger, P. T., & Thompson, K. M. (2008). Normative behavior and information: The social aspects of information access. *Library & Information Science Research, 30*(1), 56–66.

Cabral, James E., et al. (2012). Using technology to enhance access to justice. *Harvard Journal of Law & Technology, 26*(1), 241–403.

Cantrell, D. J. (2002). Justice for interests of the poor: The problem of navigating the system without counsel. *Fordham Law Review, 70,* 1573–1590.

Cappelletti, M., & Garth, B. (1978). Access to justice: The newest wave in the worldwide movement to make rights effective. *Buffalo Law Review, 27*, 181.

Carle, S. (2001). Re-valuing lawyering for middle income clients. *Fordham Law Review, 70*(3), 719.

Charn, J., & Selbin, J. (2013). The clinic lab office. *Wisconsin Law Review*, 145.

Childers, T. (1975). *The information-poor in America*. Metuchen, NJ: Scarecrow Press.

Clarke, J. A., & Borys, D. B. (2011). Usability is free: Improving efficiency by making the courts more user friendly. In National Center for State Courts, *Future Trends in State Courts 2011* (pp. 76–81). Retrieved from http://www.ncsc.org/sitecore/content/microsites/future-trends-2011/home/Specialized-Courts-Services/~/media/Microsites/Files/Future%20Trends/Author%20PDFs/Clark%20and%20Borys.ashx.

Cohen, I. G. (2013). Rationing legal services. *Journal of Legal Analysis, 5*(1), 221–307.

Cohen, S. M., & Weiss, J. (2009). Know your audience: How NYC tribunals have addressed self-represented litigants and increased access to justice. *Journal of the National Association of Administrative Law Judiciary, 29*(2), 485–514.

Corcoran, Erin B. (2012). Bypassing civil Gideon: A legislative proposal to address the rising costs and unmet legal needs of unrepresented immigrants. *West Virginia Law Review, 115*, 643–685.

Cordova, M. M. (2010). *Services for self-represented litigants: What can be done in California's appellate courts?* Master's thesis. Retrieved from http://www.csus.edu/ppa/thesis-project/bank/2009/CordovaM.pdf.

Coursey, D., & Norris, D. F. (2008). Models of e-government: Are they correct? An empirical assessment. *Public Administration Review, 68*(3), 523–536.

Creswell, J. W. (2007). *Qualitative inquiry and research design* (2nd ed.). Thousand Oaks, CA: Sage Publications.

Creswell, J. W., & Miller, D. L. (2000). Determining validity in qualitative inquiry. *Theory into Practice, 39*(3), 124–130.

Dailey, D., Bryne, A., Powell, A., Karaganis, J., & Chung, J. (2010). *Broadband adoption in low-income communities*. Social Science Research Council.

Daniel, J. (2011). *Sampling essentials: Practical guidelines for making sampling choices*. Los Angeles, CA: Sage Publications.

Davenport, D. D., Richey, J., & Westbrook, L. (2008). E-government access to social service information: State web resources for domestic violence survivors. *Journal of the American Society for Information Science and Technology, 59*(6), 903–915.

Denscombe, M. (2007). *The good research guide: For small-scale social research*. Buckingham: Open University Press.

de Róiste, M. (2013). Bringing in the users: The role for usability evaluation in eGovernment. *Government Information Quarterly, 30*(4), 441–449.

Detlor, B., Hupfer, M. E., & Ruhi, U. (2010). Internal factors affecting the adoption and use of government websites. *Electronic Government, 7*(2), 120–136.

Downs, W. (2004). *Pro se* information trends. In National Center for State Courts, *Future Trends in State Courts 2004* (pp. 127–128). Retrieved from http://cdm16501.contentdm.oclc.org/cdm/ref/collection/accessfair/id/140.

Dyer, C. R., Fairbanks, J. E., Greiner, M. L., Barron, K., Skreen, J. L., Cerrillo-Ramirez, J., & Hinsee, B. (2013). Improving access to justice: Plain language family law court forms in Washington State. *Seattle Journal for Social Justice, 11*(3), 1065–1111.

Dyson, D. D., & Schellenberg, K. (2016). Access to justice: The readability of Legal Services Corporation legal aid Internet services. *Journal of Poverty*, 1–23.

Eaton, J. T., & Holtermann, D. (2010). Limited scope representation is here. *CBA Record*, 36–41.

Eisenhardt, K. M. (1989). Building theories from case study research. *Academy of Management Review*, *14*(4), 532–550.

Eisenhardt, K. M., & Bourgeois, L. J. (1988). Politics of strategic decision making in high-velocity environments: Toward a midrange theory. *Academy of Management Journal*, *31*(4), 737–770.

Engler, R. (2006). Toward a context-based civil right to counsel through access to justice initiatives. *Clearinghouse Review Journal of Poverty Law & Policy*, *40*, 196–209.

Engler, R. (2010). Connecting self-representation to civil Gideon: What existing data reveal about when counsel is most needed. *Fordham Urban Law Journal*, *37*(1), 37–92.

Engler, R. (2011). The toughest nut: Handling cases pitting unrepresented litigants against represented ones. *Juvenile and Family Court Journal*, *62*(1), 10–31.

Federal Communications Commission. (2010). *The national broadband plan: Connecting America*. Washington, DC. Retrieved from http://www.broadband.gov.

Fernandez, A. (2007). Polling and popular culture (news, television, and film): Limitations of the use of opinion polls in assessing the public image of lawyers. *In the Public Interest: The Report and Research Papers of the Law Society of Upper Canada's Task Force on the Rule of Law and the Independence of the Bar*, 209–232.

Finney, T., & Yanovich, J. (2006). Expanding social justice through the People's Court. *Loyola of Los Angeles Law Review*, *39*(2), 769–784.

Fisher, K. E., Durrance, J. C., & Hinton, M. B. (2004). Information grounds and the use of needs-based services by immigrants in Queens, NY: A context-based outcome evaluation approach. *Journal of the American Society for Information Science and Technology*, *55*(8), 754–766.

Flaherty, Margaret B. (2002). How courts help you help yourself. *Family Court Review*, *40*(1), 91–115.

Freedman, J. B., & Henderson, J. C. (2008). Digital usage behavior: A sense making perspective. In *Proceedings of the 41st Hawaii International Conference on System Sciences*. Retrieved from http://doi.ieeecomputersociety.org/10.1109/HICSS.2008.123.

Fritschel, B. L. (2007). Trends in library collaboration to provide access to legal information. In National Center for State Courts, *Future Trends in State Courts 2007* (pp. 84–87). Retrieved from http://cdm16501.contentdm.oclc.org/cdm/ref/collection/accessfair/id/129.

Galanter, M. (2009). Access to justice in a world of expanding social capability. *Fordham Urban Law Journal*, *37*(1), 115–128.

Gardner, D. (2006). Pursuing a right to counsel in civil cases: Introduction and overview. *Clearinghouse Review Journal of Poverty Law & Policy*, *40*, 167.

Gates, Bill (1999, Oct. 4). Everyone, anytime, anywhere: The next step for technology is universal access. *Forbes Magazine*. Retrieved from https://www.microsoft.com/presspass/ofnote/10-04forbes.mspx.

Gauld, R., Goldfinch, S., & Horsburgh, S. (2010). Do they want it? Do they use it? The "demand-side" of e-government in Australia and New Zealand. *Government Information Quarterly*, *27*(2), 177–186.

George, T. P., & Wang, W. (2008). *Washington's courthouse facilitator programs for self-represented litigants in family law cases*. Washington State Center for Court Research, Administrative Office of the Courts. Retrieved from http://media.digitalarchives.wa.gov/WA.Media/do/42389F29DA1ED49342D96087FDE5E8F3.pdf.

Gershbain, N. (2016, Feb. 22). Access to justice: A social justice issue. Retrieved from http://www.huffingtonpost.ca/nikki-gershbain/canadian-social-justice_b_9290224.html.

Giddings, J., & Robertson, M. (2003). Large-scale map or the A–Z? The place of self-help services in legal aid. *Journal of Law and Society*, *30*(1), 102–119.

Glater, J. D. (2006). A broad view of access. *Loyola of Los Angeles Law Review*, *39*(2), 759–768.

Goldschmidt, J. (2002). The *pro se* litigant's struggle for access to justice: Meeting the challenge of bench and bar resistance. *Family Court Review*, *40*(1), 36–62.

Goldschmidt, J. (2008). Judicial assistance to self-represented litigants: Lessons from the Canadian experience. *Michigan State Journal of International Law*, *17*(3), 601–656.

Gomm, R. (2004). *Social research methodology: A critical introduction*. Hampshire, England: Palgrave Macmillan.

Gordon, J. R. (2001, Spring). Legal services and the digital divide. *Management Information Exchange Journal*, 46–51.

Gray, C. (2007). Reaching out or overreaching: Judicial ethics and self-represented litigants. *Journal of the National Association of Administrative Law Judiciary*, *27*(1), 97–168.

Greacen, J. M. (2002). *Self-represented litigants and court and legal services responses to their needs: What we know*. Retrieved from www.courtinfo.ca.gov/programs/equalaccess/research.htm.

Greacen, J. M. (2005). Self-represented litigants: Learning from ten years of experience in Family Courts. *The Judges Journal*, *44*, 24–33.

Greacen, J. M. (2011). *Resources to assist self-represented litigants: A fifty state review of the "state of the state."* Retrieved from http://www.msbf.org/selfhelp/GreacenReportNationalEdition.pdf.

Greacen, J. M. (2014). Self-represented litigants, the courts, and the legal profession: Myths and realities. *Family Court Review*, *52*(4), 662–669.

Greacen, J. M., & Jones, W. L. (2013). Summit on the use of technology to expand access to justice: Analytical framework. *Harvard Journal of Law & Technology Occasional Paper Series*. Retrieved from http://jolt.law.harvard.edu/symposium/articles/GreacenJones AnalyticalFramework.pdf.

Guest, G., MacQueen, K. M., & Namey, E. E. (2012). *Applied thematic analysis*. Los Angeles, CA: Sage Publications.

Hackerson, D. K. (2010). Access to justice starts in the library: The importance of competent research skills and free/low-cost research resources. *Maine Law Review*, *62*(2), 473.

Haddon, P. A. (2014). *Too many lawyers? Too few jobs? Bridging the justice gap*. Presented at American Law Institute 2014 Meeting (Washington, DC). Retrieved from http://www.law.umaryland.edu/about/features/feature0283/JusticeGap.pdf.

Hale-Janeke, A., & Blackburn, S. (2008). Law librarians and the self-represented litigant. *Legal Reference Services Quarterly*, *27*(1), 65–88.

Hamel, J., Dufour, S., & Fortin, D. (1993). *Case study methods* (Vol. 32). Newbury Park, CA: Sage Publications.

Hannaford-Agor, P., & Mott, N. (2003). Research on self-represented litigation: Preliminary results and methodological considerations. *Justice System Journal*, *24*(2), 163–181.

Helbig, N., Ramón Gil-García, J., & Ferro, E. (2009). Understanding the complexity of electronic government: Implications from the digital divide literature. *Government Information Quarterly*, *26*(1), 89–97.

Henderson, A. (2003). Meaningful access to the courts: Assessing self-represented litigants' ability to obtain a fair, inexpensive divorce in Missouri's court system. *UMKC Law Review*, *72*(2), 571–591.

Herman, M. (2007). Increasing access to justice for the self-represented through web technologies. In National Center for State Courts, *Future Trends in State Courts 2007* (pp. 29–33). Retrieved from http://cdm16501.contentdm.oclc.org/cdm/ref/collection/accessfair/id/131.

Herman, R. D., & Renz, D. O. (2008). Advancing nonprofit organizational effectiveness research and theory: Nine theses. *Nonprofit Management and Leadership, 18*(4), 399–415.

Hilbert, J. (2009). Educational workshops on settlement and dispute resolution: Another tool for self-represented litigants in family court. *Family Law Quarterly, 43*(3), 545–569.

Hogue, J., & Hineline, A. (2013). *Can translation software help legal services agencies deliver legal information more effectively in foreign languages and plain English? An evaluation of existing translation technology and recommendations for future use.* Retrieved from http://lri.lsc.gov/sites/default/files/LRI/pdf/13/TranslationSoftwareSuitabilityforPlainEnglishand-ForeignLanguageTranslationofLegalInformationPublic.pdf.

Holland, B. (2013). The Washington State limited license legal technician practice rule: A national first in access to justice. *Mississippi Law Journal, 82,* 75–130.

Hopwood, S. R. (2011). Slicing through the great legal Gordian knot: Ways to assist *pro se* litigants in their quest for justice. *Fordham Law Review, 80,* 1229–1239.

Hornsby, W. (2010). Challenging the academy to dual (perspective): The need to embrace lawyering for personal legal services. *Maryland Law Review, 70,* 420–439.

Horrigan, J. B. (2010). *Broadband adoption and use in America* (OBI Working Paper Series No. 1). Retrieved from http://online.wsj.com/public/resources/documents/FCCSurvey.pdf.

Horrigan, J. B. (2012, March 20). *Broadband adoption in 2012: Little movement since '09 & stakeholders can do more to spur adoption.* Washington, DC: Technet.

Houseman, A. W. (2001). Civil legal assistance for low-income persons: Looking back and looking forward. *Fordham Urban Law Journal, 29*(3), 1213–1243.

Houseman, A. W. (2011). *The justice gap: Civil legal assistance today and tomorrow.* Center for American Progress.

Hunter, R., Banks, C., & Giddings, J. (2009). Australian innovations in legal aid services: Lessons from an evaluation study. In *Reaching further: Innovation, access and quality in legal services,* pp. 26–46. Norwich: Stationery Office.

Institute for the Advancement of the American Legal System. (2016, May). *Cases without counsel: Our recommendations after listening to the litigants.* Retrieved from http://iaals.du.edu/sites/default/files/documents/publications/cases_without_counsel_recommendations_report.pdf.

Jaeger, P. T., & Bertot, J. C. (2011). Responsibility rolls down: Public libraries and the social and policy obligations of ensuring access to e-government and government information. *Public Library Quarterly, 30*(2), 91–116.

Jaeger, P. T., Bertot, J. C., Thompson, K. M., Katz, S. M., and DeCoster, E. J. (2012). The intersection of public policy and public access: Digital divides, digital literacy, digital inclusion, and public libraries. *Public Library Quarterly, 31*(1), 1–20.

Jaeger, P. T., Gorham, U., Bertot, J. C., & Sarin, L. C. (2014). *Public libraries, public policies, and political processes: Serving and transforming communities in times of economic and political constraint.* Lanham, MD: Rowman & Littlefield.

Jaeger, P. T., Taylor, N. G., & Gorham, U. (2015). *Libraries, human rights, and social justice: Enabling access and promoting inclusion.* Lanham, MD: Rowman & Littlefield.

Jefferson, W. B. (2013). Brennan Lecture: Liberty and justice for some; How the legal system falls short in protecting basic human rights. *New York University Law Review, 88*(3), 1953–1982.

Jennings, M., & Greiner, D. J. (2012). The evolution of unbundling in litigation matters: Three case studies and a literature review. *Denver University Law Review, 89*(4), 825–849.

Johnson, E., Jr. (2000). Equal access to justice: Comparing access to justice in the United States and other industrial democracies. *Fordham International Law Journal, 24*, S83–S110.

Johnson, E., Jr. (2009). Justice for America's poor in the year 2020: Some possibilities based on experiences here and abroad. *DePaul Law Review, 58*, 393–424.

Johnstone, Q. (2011). Law and policy issues concerning the provision of adequate legal services for the poor. *Cornell Journal of Law and Public Policy, 20*, 571–639.

Jones, Y. P. (2006). Just the facts ma'am? A contextual approach to the legal information use environment. In *Proceedings of the 6th conference on designing interactive systems* (pp. 357–359). Retrieved from http://dx.doi.org/10.1145/1142405.1142463.

Judicial Council of California. (2007). *Handling cases involving self-represented litigants: A benchguide for judicial officers*. Retrieved from http://www.courts.ca.gov/documents/benchguide_self_rep_litigants.pdf.

Kennedy, R. F. (1965). Law Day address. *University of Chicago Law School Record, 13*, 22.

Kritzer, H.M. (1999).The professions are dead, long live the professions: Legal practice in a postprofessional world. *Law & Society Review, 33*(3), 713–759.

Kritzer, H. M. (2009). Examining the real demand for legal services. *Fordham University Urban Law Journal, 37*(1), 255–272.

Landsman, S. (2009). The growing challenge of *pro se* litigation. *Lewis & Clark Law Review, 13*(2), 439–460.

Lang, D. C. (2011). Utilizing nonlawyer advocates to bridge the justice gap in America. *Widener Law Review, 17*, 289.

Lawler, M., Giddings, J., & Robertson, M. (2009). "Maybe a solicitor needs to know that sort of thing but I don't": User perspectives on the utility of legal self-help resources. In *Reaching further: Innovation, access and quality in legal services* (pp. 26–46). Norwich: Stationery Office.

Lawler, M., Giddings, J., & Robertson, M. (2012). Opportunities and limitations in the provision of self-help legal resources to citizens in need. *Windsor Yearbook of Access to Justice, 30*(1), 185.

Ledray, S. (2013). Virtual services white paper. *Harvard Journal of Law & Technology Occasional Paper Series*. Retrieved from http://jolt.law.harvard.edu/symposium/articles/Ledray-VirtualServices.pdf.

Legal Assistance of Western New York Inc. (n.d.). *The essential plain language collection for legal aid agencies*. Retrieved from http://bit.ly/1CLEH6S.

Legal Services Corporation. (n.d.). *LSC funding*. Retrieved from http://www.lsc.gov/congress/lsc-funding.

Legal Services Corporation. (n.d.). *Technology initiative grant program*. Retrieved from http://www.lsc.gov/grants-grantee-resources/our-grant-programs/tig.

Legal Services Corporation. (2007, June). *Documenting the justice gap in America*. Retrieved from http://www.lsc.gov/sites/default/files/LSC/images/justicegap.pdf.

Legal Services Corporation. (2009, Sept.). *Documenting the justice gap in America: The current unmet civil legal needs of low-income Americans*. Retrieved from http://www.lsc.gov/sites/default/files/LSC/pdfs/documenting_the_justice_gap_in_america_2009.pdf.

Legal Services Corporation. (2012, Oct.). *Report of the Pro Bono Task Force*. Retrieved from http://www.lsc.gov/sites/default/files/LSC/lscgov4/PBTF_%20Report_FINAL.pdf.

Legal Services Corporation. (2013, Dec.). *Report of the summit on the use of technology to expand access to justice.* Retrieved from http://www.lsc.gov/sites/lsc.gov/files/LSC_Tech%20 Summit%20Report_2013.pdf.

Legal Services Corporation (2014, April 14). *Glenn Rawdon, LSC Technology Program Counsel, at the White House Forum on Increasing Access to Justice, April 8, 2014.* Retrieved from http://www.lsc.gov/media-center/blog/2014/04/14/glenn-rawdons-speech-everyone-anytime-anywhere-how-technology.

Legal Services Corporation. (2014, Oct. 17). *LSC awards nearly $3.5 million in 2014 technology grants.* Retrieved from http://www.lsc.gov/media-center/press-releases/2014/lsc-awards-nearly-35-million-2014-technology-grants-legal-aid-0.

Legal Services Corporation. (2016a). *FY 2017 budget request.* Retrieved from http://www.lsc.gov/media-center/publications/fy-2017-budget-request.

Legal Services Corporation. (2016b). *Request for proposals for website assessment and evaluation services.* Retrieved from http://www.lsc.gov/sites/default/files/attach/RFP-FordFdnWebsiteEvaluator.pdf.

Legal Services National Technology Assistance Project. (n.d.). *Website functions, stakeholders, partners, and resources.* Retrieved from https://lsntap.org/node/665.

Lidman, R. (2006). Civil Gideon as a human right: Is the US going to join step with the rest of the developed world? *Temple Political & Civil Rights Law Review, 15*, 769.

Lippmann, R. (2016, March 2). *Legal Services Corporation president: U.S. has defaulted on pledge of equal justice under law.* Retrieved from http://news.stlpublicradio.org/post/legal-services-corporation-president-us-has-defaulted-pledge-equal-justice-under-law.

MacFarlane, J. (2013, May). *The national self-represented litigants project: Identifying and meeting the needs of self-represented litigants.* Retrieved from http://www.representing-yourself.com/PDF/reportM15.pdf.

Malcomson, J., & Reid, G. (2006). *BC Supreme Court Self-Help Information Centre final evaluation report.* Law Courts Education Society of BC. Retrieved from http://www.justice-education.ca/themes/framework/documents/SHC_Final_Evaluation_Sept2006.pdf.

Mancini, L. N. (2013). Increasing access to justice for all: The programs and community partnerships of the Adams-Pratt Oakland County Law Library and their impact on self-represented litigants in Southeast Michigan. *Journal of Law in Society, 14*(1), 65–82.

Maryland Access to Justice Commission. (2012, Nov.). *Writing for self-represented litigants: A guide for Maryland's courts and civil legal services providers.* Retrieved from http://mdcourts.gov/mdatjc/pdfs/writingforsrls.pdf.

Maryland Judiciary. (2007, Aug.). *Clearing a path to justice: A report of the Maryland Judiciary Work Group on Self-Representation in the Maryland Courts.* Retrieved from http://www.courts.state.md.us/publications/pdfs/selfrepresentation0807.pdf.

Maryland Judiciary (Court Information Office). (2008, Jan.). *People's Law Library website finds permanent home with Maryland State Law Library* [document on file with the author].

Massachusetts Supreme Judicial Court Steering Committee on Self-Represented Litigants. (2008, Nov. 21). *Addressing the needs of self-represented litigants in our courts.* Retrieved from http://www.mass.gov/courts/docs/sjc/docs/self-rep-final-report.pdf.

Melton, L., Snider O., & Zorza, R. (2005). *Ensuring the long term viability of the statewide website component of the access to justice system: The final report of the website sustainability project.* Retrieved from http://lsntap.org/sites/all/files/websiteSustainReportSept2005.pdf.

Menkel-Meadow, C. (1984). Legal aid in the United States: The professionalization and politicization of legal services in the 1980's. *Osgoode Hall Law Journal, 22*, 29.

Migration Policy Institute. (2011, Dec.). *LEP Data Brief.* Retrieved from http://www.migrationpolicy.org/research/limited-english-proficient-individuals-united-states-number-share-growth-and-linguistic.

Miles, M. B., Huberman, A. M., & Saldaña, J. (2014). *Qualitative data analysis: A methods sourcebook.* Thousand Oaks, CA: Sage Publications.

Mindlin, M. (2005). Is plain language better? Comparative study of plain language court forms. *Scribes Journal of Legal Writing, 10*, 55.

Morino, M. (2011). Leap of reason: Managing to outcomes in an era of scarcity. *Innovations, 6*(3), 167–177.

Morris, V. (2013). Navigating justice: Self-help resources, access to justice and whose job is it anyway? *Mississippi Law Journal, 82*, 162–181.

National Center for Education Statistics. (n.d.). *State and county estimates of low literacy: FAQs.* Retrieved from https://nces.ed.gov/naal/estimates/FAQ.aspx.

National Center for State Courts. (2006). Access to justice: The self-represented litigant. In National Center for State Courts, *Future Trends in State Courts 2006* (p. 18–19). Retrieved from http://ncsc.contentdm.oclc.org/cdm/singleitem/collection/accessfair/id/135.

National Center for State Courts. (2012, Nov.). *Access brief 1: Self-help services.* Retrieved from http://cdm16501.contentdm.oclc.org/utils/getfile/collection/accessfair/id/263/filename/264.pdf.

National Center for State Courts. (2013, July). *Access to justice for limited English proficient litigants: Creating solutions to language barriers in state courts.* http://www.ncsc.org/services-and-experts/areas-of-expertise/language-access/~/media/files/pdf/services%20and%20experts/areas%20of%20expertise/language%20access/call-to-action.ashx.

National Center for State Courts. (2014, July). *Access brief: Access to justice commissions.* Retrieved from https://www.ncsc.org/~/media/Microsites/Files/access/NSCS%20brief%20ATJ%20Commissions%20updated%207-3-14.ashx.

National Legal Aid and Defender Association. (n.d.). History of civil legal aid. Retrieved from http://www.nlada.org/About/About_HistoryCivil.

National Telecommunications and Information Administration. (2013a, June). *Household broadband adoption climbs to 72.4 percent.* Retrieved from http://www.ntia.doc.gov/blog/2013/household-broadband-adoption-climbs-724-percent.

National Telecommunications and Information Administration. (2013b, May). *U.S. broadband availability: June 2010–June 2012.* Retrieved from http://www.ntia.doc.gov/files/ntia/publications/usbb_avail_report_05102013.pdf.

Newton, N. (2010). *The use of semi-structured interviews in qualitative research: Strengths and weaknesses.* Retrieved from https://www.academia.edu/1561689/The_use_of_semi-structured_interviews_in_qualitative_research_strengths_and_weaknesses.

Owens, D. S. (2013). The reality of *pro se* representation. *Mississippi Law Journal, 82*, 147–160.

Pantzer, D. (2016). Public legal information as common ground for the justice community. In National Center for State Courts, *Future Trends in State Courts 2016* (pp. 61–65). Retrieved from https://www.ncsc.org/~/media/Microsites/Files/Trends%202016/Trends-2016-low.ashx.

Patton, M. Q. (1987). *How to use qualitative methods in evaluation.* Newbury Park, CA: Sage Publications.

Patton, M. Q. (2002). *Qualitative evaluation and research methods* (3rd ed.). Thousand Oaks, CA: Sage Publications.

Pearce, R. G. (2004). Redressing inequality in the market for justice: Why access to lawyers will never solve the problem and why rethinking the role of judges will help. *Fordham Law Review, 73*, 969–981.

Penna, R. M. (2011). *The nonprofit outcomes toolbox*. Hoboken, NJ: Wiley.

Perrin, A., & Duggan, M. (2015, June). *Americans' Internet Access: 2000–2015*. Pew Research Center. Retrieved from http://www.pewinternet.org/2015/06/26/americans-internet-access-2000-2015.

Pettigrew, K. E., Durrance, J. C., & Unruh, K. T. (2002). Facilitating community information seeking using the Internet: Findings from three public library-community network systems. *Journal of the American Society for Information Science and Technology, 53*(11), 894–903.

Pettinato, T. R. (2008). Dealing with *pro se* patrons. *Public Services Quarterly, 4*(3), 283–289.

Pietersen, W., Ebbers, W., & van Dijk, J. (2007). Personalization in the public sector: An inventory of organizational and user obstacles towards personalization of electronic services in the public sector. *Government Information Quarterly, 24*(1), 148–164.

Plain Language Action and Information Network. (2011, May). *Federal plain language guidelines*. Retrieved from http://www.plainlanguage.gov/howto/guidelines/FederalPLGuidelines/FederalPLGuidelines.pdf.

Pollock, J. (2015, Feb. 4). "You have a right to a lawyer . . . if you can afford it": A look at the history of the right to counsel in civil cases and the current efforts to expand it. *Bloomberg BNA, 81*(48).

Rasch, M. (2011). A new public interest appellate model: Public counsel's court-based self-help clinic and pro bono "triage" for indigent *pro se* civil litigants on appeal. *Journal of Appellate Practice & Process*, 11. Retrieved from http://works.bepress.com/meehan_rasch/4.

Real, B., McDermott, A., Bertot, J. C., & Jaeger, P. T. (2015). Digital inclusion and the Affordable Care Act: Public libraries, politics, policy, and enrollment in "Obamacare." *Public Library Quarterly, 34*(1), 1–22.

Reddick, C. G. (2005). Citizen interaction with e-government: From the streets to servers? *Government Information Quarterly, 22*(1), 38–57.

Rembold, J. L. (2014). Connecting communities with health insurance: Public libraries and the Affordable Care Act. *Indiana Libraries, 33*(2), 50–52.

Rhode, D. L. (2001). Access to justice. *Fordham Law Review, 69*(5), 1785–1819.

Rhode, D. L. (2004). Access to justice: Again, still. *Fordham Law Review, 73*(3), 1013–1029.

Rhode, D. L. (2009). Whatever happened to access to justice. *Loyola of Los Angeles Law Review, 42*, 869–912.

Rhode, D. L. (2013). Access to justice: An agenda for legal education and research. *Journal of Legal Education, 62*(4), 531–550.

Rhode, D. L., & Bam, D. (2012). *A roadmap to justice*. Retrieved from http://papers.ssrn.com/sol3/papers.cfm?abstract_id=2025109.

Ridge, J. B. (2010). *Evaluation techniques for difficult to measure programs*. Bloomington, IN: Xlibris Corporation.

Robinson, J. P., DiMaggio, P., & Hargittai, E. (2003). New social survey perspectives on the digital divide. *IT & Society, 1*(5), 1–22.

Rosenberg, T. (2016, June 1). Legal aid with a twist. *New York Times*. Retrieved from http://www.nytimes.com/2016/06/01/opinion/legal-aid-with-a-digital-twist.html?emc=eta1&_r=0.

Rossi, P. H., & Freeman, H. E. (1989). *Evaluation: A systematic approach.* Newbury Park, CA: Sage Publications.

Rothman, R. A. (1984). Deprofessionalization: The case of law in America. *Work and Occupations, 11*(2), 183–206.

Royse, D., Thyer, B., & Padgett, D. (2009). *Program evaluation: An introduction.* Cengage Learning.

Rulli, L. S. (2011). On the road to civil Gideon: Give lessons from the enactment of a right to counsel for indigent homeowners in federal civil forfeiture proceedings. *Journal of Law & Policy, 19,* 683.

Ryan, G. W., & Bernard, H. R. (2003). Techniques to identify themes. *Field Methods, 15*(1), 85–109.

Sandefur, R. L. (2014). *Accessing justice in the contemporary USA: Findings from the Community Needs and Services Survey.* Retrieved from http://papers.ssrn.com/sol3/papers.cfm?abstract_id=2478040.

Sandefur, R. L., & Smyth, A. (2011). *Access across America: First report of the Civil Justice Infrastructure Mapping Project.* Retrieved from http://papers.ssrn.com/sol3/papers.cfm?abstract_id=1962790.

Saxton, M. L., Naumer, C. M., & Fisher, K. E. (2007). 2-1-1 information services: Outcomes assessment, benefit-cost analysis, and policy issues. *Government Information Quarterly, 24*(1), 186–215.

Schauffler, R., & Strickland, S. (2015). The case for counting cases. *Court Review, 51,* 52.

Schneider, R. K. (2011). Illiberal construction of *pro se* pleadings. *University of Pennsylvania Law Review, 159,* 585–633.

Schwarz, C. D. (2004). *Pro se* divorce litigants. *Family Court Review, 42*(4), 655–672.

Scott, S. (2000). Law online. *Alternative Law Journal, 25,* 24–28.

Seidman, J. (2006). *Interviewing as qualitative research: A guide for researchers in education and the social sciences.* New York: Teachers College Press.

Selbin, J., Charn, J., Alfieri, A. V., & Wizner, S. (2012). Service delivery, resource allocation and access to justice: Greiner and Pattanayak and the research imperative. *Yale Law Journal Online, 122,* 45–67. http://dx.doi.org/10.2139/ssrn.2003960.

Self-Represented Litigation Network. (2008). *Best practices in court-based programs for the self-represented: Concepts, attributes, issues for exploration, examples, contacts and resources.* Retrieved from http://ncsc.contentdm.oclc.org/cdm/ref/collection/accessfair/id/3na28.

Self-Represented Litigation Network. (2014). *Library self-help programs and services: A survey of law library programs for self-represented litigants, including self-help centers.* Retrieved from http://www.srln.org/node/551/survey-srln-library-working-group-national-self-help-libraries-survey-srln-2013.

Shepard, R. T. (2010). The self-represented litigant: Implications for the bench and bar. *Family Court Review, 48*(4), 607–618.

Sim, S. C., & Rocha, K. A. (1998). A qualitative and quantitative approach in evaluating a telephone based information and referral program. *Information and Referral, 20,* 1–14.

Slack, F., & Rowley, J. (2004). Challenges in the delivery of e-government through kiosks. *Journal of Information Science, 30,* 369–377.

Smith, A. (2015, April 1). *U.S. smartphone use in 2015. Pew Research Center.* Retrieved from http://www.pewinternet.org/2015/04/01/us-smartphone-use-in-2015.

Smith, L. F., & Stratford, B. (2012). DIY in family law: A case study of a brief advice clinic for *pro se* litigants. *Journal of Law & Family Studies, 14*(2), 167–277.

Smith, R. (2013). *Can digital replace personal in the delivery of legal aid?* Retrieved from http://www.ilagnet.org/jscripts/tiny_mce/plugins/filemanager/files/The_Hague_2013/Session_Papers/5.1_-_Roger_Smith.pdf>.

Smith, R. H. (1919). *Justice and the poor*. The Carnegie Foundation for the Advancement of Teaching.

Snukals, B. W., & Sturtevant, G. H., Jr. (2007). *Pro se* litigation: Best practices from a judge's perspective. *University of Richmond Law Review, 42*, 93–105.

Spieler, E. A. (2013). The paradox of access to civil justice: The "glut" of new lawyers and the persistence of unmet need. *University of Toledo Law Re*view, *44*, 101–139.

Spira, D. (2009). Dealing with the problems of *pro se*: The settlement assistance program in the Northern District of Illinois. *Holy Cross Journal of Law & Public Policy, 13*, 185–222.

Stake, R. E. (1995). *The art of case study research*. Thousand Oaks, CA: Sage Publications.

State Justice Institute. (n.d.). *About SJI*. Retrieved from http://www.sji.gov/about-sji.

State Justice Institute. (2014). New report by the Court Statistics Project provides additional resources. *E-SJI News, 24*(4), 3.

State of New Hampshire Judicial Branch. (2004). *Challenge to justice: A report on self-represented litigants in New Hampshire courts, findings and recommendations of the New Hampshire Supreme Court Task Force on Self-Representation*. Retrieved from http://www.courts.state.nh.us/supreme/prosereport.pdf.

Staudt, R. W. (2005). Technology for justice customers: Bridging the digital divide facing self-represented litigants. *University of Maryland Law Journal of Race, Religion, Gender & Class, 5*, 71–94.

Staudt, R. W. (2009). All the wild possibilities: Technology that attacks barriers to access to justice. *Loyola of Los Angeles Law Review, 42*, 101–129.

Staudt, R. W. (2013). Access to justice and technology clinics: A 4% solution (with Andrew P. Medeiros) (symposium). *Chicago-Kent Law Review, 88*(3), 695–727. Retrieved from http://scholarship.kentlaw.iit.edu/fac_schol/784.

Staudt, R. W., & Hannaford, P. L. (2002). Access to justice for the self-represented litigant: An interdisciplinary investigation by designers and lawyers. *Syracuse Law* Review, *52*, 1017–1047.

Steinberg, J. (2011). In pursuit of justice? Case outcomes and the delivery of unbundled legal services. *Georgetown Journal on Poverty Law Policy, 18*(3), 453–505.

Stenbacka, C. (2001). Qualitative research requires quality concepts of its own. *Management Decision, 39*(7), 551–555.

Stout Risius Ross. (2016, March 16). *The financial cost and benefits of establishing a right to counsel in eviction proceedings under Intro 214-A*. Presented for Pro Bono and Legal Services Committee of the New York City Bar Association. Retrieved from http://www2.nycbar.org/pdf/report/uploads/SRR_Report_Financial_Cost_and_Benefits_of_Establishing_a_Right_to_Counsel_in_Eviction_Proceedings.pdf.

Struffolino, M. N. (2012). Taking limited representation to the limits: The efficacy of using unbundled legal services in domestic-relations matters involving litigation. *St. Mary's Journal on Legal Malpractice & Ethics, 2*, 166.

Swank, D. A. (2004). The *pro se* phenomenon. *BYU Journal of Public Law, 19*, 373–386.

Tait, K. (2011). Effective communication with self-represented litigants. *Case in Point, 2011*, 12–15. Retrieved from http://www.judges.org/pdf/caseinpoint_2011.pdf.

Taylor, N. G., Gorham, U., Jaeger, P. T., & Bertot, J. C. (2014). IT and collaborative community services: The roles of the public library, local government, and nonprofit entity partnerships. *International Journal of Public Administration in the Digital Age, 1*(1), 91–107.

Taylor, R. S. (1991). Information use environments. *Progress in Communication Sciences, 10* (217), 55.

Thompson, K. M., Jaeger, P. T., Taylor, N. G., Subramaniam, M., & Bertot, J. C. (2014). *Digital literacy and digital inclusion: Information policy and the public library*. Lanham, MD: Rowman & Littlefield.

Tomer, A., & Kane, J. (2015, December). *Broadband adoption rates and gaps in U.S. metropolitan areas*. Brookings Institute.

Udell, D. S., & Diller, R. (2007). Access to the courts: An essay for the Georgetown University Law Center Conference on the Independence of the Courts. *Georgetown Law Journal, 95*, 1127–1154.

Urban Insight. (2016). *Best practice benchmarking for legal services websites 2016*. Retrieved from https://www.urbaninsight.com/2016/01/14/best-practice-benchmarking-for-legal-services-websites-2016.

Van Wormer, N. I. (2007). Help at your fingertips: A twenty-first century response to the *pro se* phenomenon. *Vanderbilt Law Review, 60*(3), 983–1019.

Verdegem, P., & Verleye, G. (2009). User-centered e-government in practice: A comprehensive model for measuring user satisfaction. *Government Information Quarterly, 26*(3), 487–497.

Warren, G. (2004). Reaching out to self-represented litigants through virtual reference and education. In National Center for State Courts, *Future Trends in State Courts 2004* (pp. 95–96). Retrieved from http://ncsc.contentdm.oclc.org/cdm/ref/collection/accessfair/id/138.

Washington State Access to Justice Board. (2004). *Access to justice technology principles*. Retrieved from http://www.courts.wa.gov/court_rules/?fa=court_rules.display&group=am&set=ATJ&ruleid=amatj01order.

Weber, M. (2007). *Pro Bono Net Circuit Rider program evaluation* [document on file with the author].

Westbrook, L. (2008). E-government support for people in crisis: An evaluation of police department website support for domestic violence survivors using "person-in-situation" information need analysis. *Library & Information Science Research, 30*(1), 22–38.

Westbrook, L. (2009). Crisis information concerns: Information needs of domestic violence survivors. *Information Processing & Management, 45*(1), 98–114.

Widdison, R. (2013). Electronic paths to Justice. *Journal of Information, Law and Technology (JILT), 2*(3).

Wolf, M. J. (2012). Collaborative technology improves access to justice. *New York University Journal of Legislation & Public Policy, 15*, 759–789.

World Bank. (n.d.). *Definition of e-government*. Retrieved from http://go.worldbank.org/M1JHE0Z280.

Yaniv, O. (2005). Immigrants warned on green card cons. *New York Daily News*, October 19. Available: http://articles.nydailynews.com/2005-10-19/local/18313877_1_immigrants-application-eligible-countries.

Yin, R. K. (2009). *Case study research: Design and methods* (4th ed.). Thousand Oaks, CA: Sage Publications.

Yin, R. K. (2011). *Applications of case study research* (3rd ed.). Thousand Oaks, CA: Sage Publications.

Yu, L. (2011). The divided views of the information and digital divides: A call for integrative theories of information inequality. *Journal of Information Science, 37*(6), 660–679.

Zickuhr, K. (2013, Sept.). *Who's not online and why*. Pew Internet & American Life Project. Retrieved from http://www.pewinternet.org/files/old-media//Files/Reports/2013/PIP_Offline%20adults_092513_PDF.pdf.

Zimerman, N., & Tyler, T. R. (2010). Between access to counsel and access to justice: A psychological perspective. *Fordham Urban Law Journal, 37*, 473–507.

Zorza, R. (2004). The disconnect between the requirements of judicial neutrality and those of the appearance of neutrality when parties appear *pro se*: Causes, solutions, recommendations, and implications. *Georgetown Journal of Legal Ethics, 17*, 423–454.

Zorza, R. (2007). Spreading and adopting best practices for court-based programs for self-represented litigants. In National Center for State Courts, *Future Trends in State Courts 2007* (p. 81–83). Retrieved from http://ncsc.contentdm.oclc.org/cdm/ref/collection/accessfair/id/130.

Zorza, Richard. (2009a). An overview of self-represented litigation innovation, its impact, and an approach for the future: An invitation to dialogue. *Family Law Quarterly, 43*(3), 519–542.

Zorza, R. (2009b). Self-represented litigants and the access to justice revolution in the state courts: Cross-pollinating perspectives toward a dialogue for innovation in the courts and the administrative law system. *Journal of the National Association of Administrative Law Judiciary, 29*(1), 63–91.

Zorza, R. (2010). Access to justice: The emerging consensus and some questions and implications. *Judicature, 94*(4), 156–167.

Zorza, R. (2012a). The access to justice "sorting hat": Towards a system of triage and intake that maximizes access and outcomes. *Denver University Law Review, 89*, 859–886.

Zorza, R. (2012b, April). *The sustainable 21st century law library: Vision, deployment and assessment for access to justice.* Retrieved from http://www.zorza.net/LawLibrary.pdf.

Zorza, R., & Horowitz, D. J. (2006). The Washington State access to justice technology principles: A perspective for justice system professionals. *Justice System Journal, 27*(3), 248–267.

Index

Page references for figures are italicized

About the Author

Ursula Gorham, Ph.D., J.D., is a lecturer in the College of Information Studies at the University of Maryland. She is admitted to practice law in Maryland and previously served as a law clerk in Maryland appellate and federal bankruptcy courts. Dr. Gorham's research spans the role of libraries in public policy and political processes; access to legal information and court documents; and collaborative efforts among libraries, community organizations, and government agencies to meet the information needs of underserved populations. Her research has been published in the *Law Library Journal*, *Government Information Quarterly*, *Public Library Quarterly*, the *Journal of Education for Library and Information Science*, the *Journal of Open Access to Law*, *Information Polity*, and *First Monday*. She is a co-author of *Public Libraries, Public Policies, and Political Processes: Serving and Transforming Communities in Times of Economic and Political Constraint* (2014) and *Libraries, Human Rights, and Social Justice: Enabling Access and Promoting Inclusion* (2015). In addition, she currently serves as an associate editor of *Library Quarterly*.

Lightning Source UK Ltd.
Milton Keynes UK
UKOW04n0743190717
305564UK00001B/4/P

9 781442 270299